Hip Girl's Handbook for the Working World

Also by Jennifer Musselman and Patty DeGregori Fletcher:

The Hip Girl's Handbook for Home, Car, & Money Stuff

Hip Girl's Handbook for the Working World

Jennifer Musselman
With Patty Fletcher

WILDCAT CANYON PRESS
An Imprint of Council Oak Books
San Francisco / Tulsa

Wildcat Canyon Press
An Imprint of Council Oak Books, Tulsa, OK 74104
www.counciloakbooks.com

Printed in the United States of America

Interior design by Margaret Copeland
Cover design by Buffy Terry

Library of Congress Cataloging-in-Publication Data

Musselman, Jennifer, 1973-
 Hip girls handbook for the working world / Jennifer Musselman with Patty
Fletcher.— 1st ed.
     p. cm.
 ISBN 1-885171-84-6
1. Vocational guidance for women. 2. Career development. 3. Women—
Employment. I. Fletcher, Patty, 1975- II. Title.
 HF5382.6.M87 2005
 650.1'082—dc22
                                     2004029796

"Every blade of grass has
its angel that bends over
it and whispers, 'Grow, grow.'"
— THE TALMUD

This book is dedicated to my angel, Roy M. Carlisle.

Table of Contents

Part One — Seizing Success

Part Two — Gettin' Jiggy on the Job

Part Three — Get a Clue & Get a Life

Acknowledgments

It was August 2004, and my life would be changed forever. I had just begun writing this book and, little did I know, a new chapter in my life. The completion of this book is proof that I am blessed with a strong support group. Without them, this book would certainly not have been possible.

First, my deepest gratitude to my new friend Kelly Wellman, who, through compassion and tough love, has helped me "rewrite" my future. Thank you for serving as a mirror, forcing me to truly see, for once, the reflection that stands before me. I love what I see!

The simple words "thank you" alone cannot express my love and appreciation for my dearest friends Mary Catherine Filar, Marisa Becerra, Patty Fletcher, Kim Bloom, Clint Taylor, Eva Kolacz, Jen Benito, Linda Hunter and Susan Downs, who were strong for me when I, for the first time in a very long time, couldn't be strong for myself. Through despair, I was reminded what authentic love is. It's lying next to me stroking my hair as I lay curled on my bed in a ball of gut-wrenching pain. It's sharing in compassion-filled email exchanges and phone calls that let me regurgitate my agony time and time again. It's bringing me food and forcing me to eat when all I wanted to do was sleep my hurt away. It's holding my hand as I begrudgingly ventured outside of my cave when all I wanted to do was cry and forget I'd ever felt this way. Collectively, you gave me a gift almost greater than your love; you enabled and encouraged my metamorphosis into a woman who finds strength in my vulnerability as much as my independence.

To my other close group of friends, both old and new, thank you for pushing past my pride and encircling me with a warm, safe cocoon.

And, of course, God bless my family for being my biggest cheerleaders. I hope you feel my presence deep within your soul as I feel yours, despite the distance.

Much of this little career handbook's foundation (and tidbits about life, love and friendships) was sculpted from the miraculous eight years I've shared with my extended family at MTV Networks. The individuals who make up my Nickelodeon Communications team in particular have been unknowingly instrumental in shaping my journey as a professional and as a woman of compassion. I must, however, specifically acknowledge Marianne Romano, who was blindsided years ago with the responsibility of taming this lion. I'm in awe of your patience and am forever grateful for your faith in me. The lessons you've taught me, and those tough ones we've learned and have grown from together, extend well beyond the walls of my office with a bathroom window.

Mrs. Paula Filar, your human resources expertise and sound advice has been invaluable to this book. Now your working wisdom can serve to empower women everywhere to take charge of their careers, much like your own story of independence and career success has impressed me for so long. You and your entire family have always been so gracious to me out of the kindness of your hearts, and I feel lucky to have you all in my life.

A hearty thank you to the many gals who let me recount their stories of fear, desperation, embarrassment and vulnerabilities. To my contributor, Mrs. Patty Fletcher, and her parents who both continue to offer a wealth of wisdom and support for the good of our books.

And, of course, a huge, gigantic thank you to Ja-lene Clark and Paulette Millichap. You both have been such a gift from God for Patty and me to work with! Thank you for believing in and supporting our vision.

It is with great satisfaction (and a bit of amazement) that I finally hit "Enter" on the last few lines of this book. Without a doubt, this moment has finally arrived, ultimately, because of God's strength and love for me. I anxiously look forward to not just living, but seeking and embracing with all my heart, mind and soul, the next chapter God has drafted for me to claim as my own.

Authors' Note

The *Hip Girl's Handbook for the Working World* is your one-stop shopping guide for navigating through the unwritten, indefinable and far too often unspoken "rules" for kick-starting, strategizing and dealing with career-related issues and opportunities we gals face in today's workforce. Our book is an overview of years of tried and tested approaches to life/work situations and important employment jargon that your high school or college education didn't teach (or if they did, you were too busy sleeping through it). When reading our book, recognize that we use the terms client, vendor, customer or boss generically. You, the reader, should apply the term to your individual field. For instance, if you're a teacher, your "clients" are your students and parents, and if you're a flight attendant, your "customers" are your passengers.

Our HipTips direct you to plenty of niche-specific resources in the event you have a particular situation that requires more in-depth studying. Try the book's information on for size for all of your different career needs. Use the book like you use that must-have black dress you can wear to almost anything. Add your own "accessories" that will make the book's advice fit the event, industry or your personal needs.

We feel it's especially important to specifically address the *Gettin' Jiggy on the Job* section. Not all men — husbands, boyfriends or bachelors — are created equal (take Brad Pitt as a prime example!). Besides appearances, they each come to the table with their own approaches to life matters. The same is true of bosses, clients, subordinates and coworkers. You'll hate or love (or grow to do both) some of their individual styles and traits. Then you'll have to carefully pick and choose what you can learn to live with or compromise on for the sake of achieving the same goals. And if the overall package can't meet your most important needs, you may have to kick 'em to the curb. So, like in love, recognize some bosses, co-workers and clients might require a little patience, attention and stroking of egos to make your job the opportunity you've been dreaming of. Or at the very least, like in the case of a Mr. Right Now, use your work as a stepping-stone.

In "The Basics" and "Foreplay for Fair Play" chapters, exercise your resourcefulness, especially in extreme measures of doubt or fear, such as sexual harassment or race discrimination. We are not lawyers, so consult an attorney immediately for your protection. Laws are ever-changing and differ from state to state. Therefore it's important to investigate the laws that apply to you and your situation before you find yourself in the middle of litigation. The same is true of many corporate or organizational employee benefits packages. We offer the general foundation to help you better understand what your company offers. But each policy is different. Know how yours works.

And don't just take our word for it. Do your homework for your industry's standards. For more in-depth facts about some of the issues covered in this book, check out some of the resources in our bibliography and throughout the book in our HipTips. They're all great sources of information. And once you get the basics here, hopefully understanding their material will be easier.

Hip Girls Talk Shop

Put your plungers and car jacks down for a second and grab your high heels and briefcases. We Hip Girls are taking you on the shopping spree of a lifetime in the mega-mall for career success.

Whether you're entering the work force for the first time, are currently enveloped in the politics of business, or are in dire need of a career make-over, *The Hip Girl's Handbook for the Working World* is your one-stop-shopping guide for successfully managing your professional journey.

Our trailblazing "fore-sisters" who pioneered our right to work outside the home fought massive struggles to lay the foundation for an infrastructure of life choices for us all. Thanks to them and generations of women thereafter (and some smart and upstanding men who recognize we're just as capable, intelligent and competitive — only prettier!) who continue to champion our cause, we women can trade in our aprons for a suit, lab coat or police uniform, enjoy them both, or put our careers on hold to become full-time mothers without regret.

From the women who are their family's house managers to the single gals who support themselves as teachers, doctors, corporate executives, administrative assistants, fashionistas or politicians, we all face similar job-related issues. Management style and financial decisions plague most of us at one time or another. It's how we deal with them where we truly differ. We all may question our success and whether or not the sacrifice is worth it, whether you're a work-at-home mom who longs for adult conversation, or a busy, high-paid attorney who's missing the all-girls trip to Hawaii. And probably the most universal question of all is, — what ever do we wear to the interview, field trip or meeting?

Yep. Our *Wonder Woman*, *Legally Blonde* and *Charlie's Angels* dreams sure can be tricky to attain. (Seriously, who can really work that hard and look that good at the end of every day?) But with a little insight from people who have been there, done that, and are all the wiser to the women still climbing the ladder, collaboratively, we can bring a valuable career tool to the table: our personal experiences of triumphs and failures.

So heed to the powerful knowledge found in this book. Then tailor the information to inspire your own stories of professional and personal success. After all, it's your life, your career and your personal happiness at stake . . . priceless commodities well worth the risk!

PART ONE

---===oooo===---

Seizing Success

Whether you're currently climbing your way to the top or scratching at the back door trying to get in, don't let signing on the dotted line or fancy terms like 'PPO' and 'stock options' get you frazzled. The following pages offer relief (and clarification) on everything from negotiating your promotion, picking and choosing your health-related and financial options to just what outfit will rock your presentation.

The Basics:

A Foundation for Getting Your Foot in the Door

"As a manager, I do my fair share of hiring and am constantly bewildered by how potential employees represent themselves. Some come in for interviews so laid back that I think they're not really interested in the job. One woman recently had the audacity within the first 15 minutes of the interview to ask me if our payroll department was in-house or outsourced. She wanted to know how hard it would be to get an issue resolved if there was a mistake on her paycheck. I thought, 'WHAT!?!? Try getting the job first, dingbat!'"

—Julie, 28, Regional Manager for a Fortune 500
Computer Software Company

Rock 'em with Your Résumé

Your résumé (otherwise known as your CV — Curriculum Vitae — in the educational system and in many other countries) is your representative to the business world. It speaks for you when you can't do it for yourself. Whether you're applying to be the next Bachelorette or to be a pilot for American Airlines , your résumé should highlight your superior qualifications. A résumé's purpose is to show your potential employer that you've got most of "the goods" he's looking for in an employee. Once you've nailed the interview, your résumé reinforces you've got what it takes above your competition. Below are the basic steps for organizing your ideas for the résumé-writing process.

◆ **List your personal contact information at the top.** This includes your professional name, daytime and cell phone numbers, snail mail and professional email addresses. Make sure your contact information is appropriate for your audience. For instance, skip nicknames that may sound immature or present a party-like connotation, like Jo-Jo or Susie. Establish an email account that is professional in tone, like SusanB@yahoo.com, and keep your HotMama4U@aol.com address strictly for your friends.

◆ **Identify your objective.** What is it that you want? Know. Be clear, brief and specific. Do not show your own confusion by over-generalizing or stating a lot about nothing. If you aren't certain, at least point the person reading it in the right direction of your interest.

  ☐ **Bad example:** *Objective:* Seeking a full-time position in an industry that utilizes my strong people skills, self-motivating personality and communications degree.

  ☐ **Good example:** *Objective:* To secure an associate position in the real estate industry with a high-volume, reputable agency.

Hip Tip   *Prepare different résumés tailored to different industries or job functions. Specifically, tweak your objective and highlight certain qualifications or skills that meet the posted requirements for a potential job applicant on the online job board or employment Websites that you're searching.*

◆ **Next, organize the content of your résumé** so that your superior skills and experience stand out in a crowd (just like you'd do when choosing your work-out outfit to bait and snag the hot guy at your gym). Do you speak another language, or are you proficient with Excel software? Include this, but keep your style professional, concise and poignant.

    □   Arrange your résumé chronologically. List your most recent work experience — including the company name, town/state, position and responsibilities — at the top, with the older work experience listed last. If you're looking for a new position not related to your most recent job, organize your résumé in the skill style below. In chronological résumés, don't list a job as a bartender or babysitter if it is not relevant to the job you're applying for unless you can't sufficiently explain chunks of unemployment with reasons like school, a year-long excursion abroad or time off due to child rearing.

    □   Skill-related ordering. Generally speaking, it's smart to stick with chronological ordering. But skill-related ordering works well if you have chunks of time where you didn't work, were job or field hopping, or have limited work experience overall. In skill-related ordering, divide your experience according to similar responsibilities like administrative, management or more creative endeavors. For example:

WRITING EXPERIENCE

Magazines

Sr. Editor, *SNAP Magazine*, NY, NY
(Jan. '02 – Present)

Freelance Feature Writer, *IMAGE Magazine*, Chicago, IL
(Feb. '00 – Jan. '02)

Books

AUTHOR: *The Hip Girl's Handbook for the Working World*
(April '05)

CO-AUTHOR: *The Hip Girl's Handbook for Home, Car & Money Stuff*
(Aug. '03)

PUBLIC RELATIONS EXPERIENCE

Manager, Smith and Jones Public Relations, Chicago, IL
(Sept. '00 – Jan. '02)

Consultant, Nordstrom's, NY, NY
(May '98 – Sept. '00)

◆ **Next, list your education.** Start with your highest degree first. If you've earned a degree or prominent certification higher than your high school diploma, drop your diploma or GED from your résumé. If you have limited work experience, add exemplary honors like graduating magna cum laude or receiving a prestigious award or scholarship. Feel free to leave out the year you earned your degree or certification if you think it might be construed negatively, meaning you may appear too old or too young for the position. For example:

B.A./Fashion, University of Minnesota at Minneapolis, 2004 (magna cum laude)

Fashion Institute Color Certification, Los Angeles, CA (Stylist of the Year)

Hip Tip *Your résumé is documentation for the human resources department or superintendent board to refer to when monitoring your performance or researching whether to hire you. Plain and simple: Don't lie about your educational achievements or work responsibilities. If you attended college but dropped out the last semester to pursue your acting ambitions, acknowledge your schooling efforts, but don't list a degree you never earned. Likewise, don't be overly generous with job responsibilities by misrepresenting your role as the leader of the firm's success, when actually you held a support position.*

◆ **Now, close your rock-solid résumé** by boasting about your skills, professional memberships, related activities and volunteerism. Girl, if you don't, no one else will. Just make sure to back up your claims with proof. (If you say you fluently speak three languages, be prepared to show off your talents when you least expect it.) If you're an aspiring actress, this is one of your most valuable assets because it shows your versatility.

◆ **Lastly, review your résumé** for major no-no's and cut and delete wherever possible. If it's more than one page, shorten it. Spell-check and review your grammar. Are your sentences complete and to the point? Now's not the time to infuse your sense of humor because it won't translate well on paper.

Hip Tip Is your page still blank after spending two hours trying to compile and organize your thoughts? Check out the link http://office. microsoft.com/en-us/templates/CT061993551033.aspx. Microsoft offers a cornucopia of résumé and cover letter templates for you to download, including formats that are industry- or situation-specific. All you have to do is plug in your information. If you're stuck determining what skills to highlight or deciding what résumé styles cater to your career, see your professor or a career counselor. A list of Master Career Counselors and Master Career Development Professionals in your state can be accessed at the Website of the National Career Development Association: www.ncda.org or toll-free: 866.367.6232. If you'd rather let your fingers do the walking, check out your local yellow pages and search categories such as "career counseling," "vocational counseling," or "employment counseling."

The Cover Letter — Your Résumé's Gift-Wrapping

When soliciting someone for a job, don't send a naked résumé. Dress it up with a letter at the front introducing yourself. This is the cover letter. It's the pretty gift-wrapping your potential employer quickly tears through before getting to the goods: you!

◆ **Start by listing your contact information** in the upper right-hand corner of the page. Give your name, mailing address, phone and email.

◆ **Next, skip to the left side of the page to type the date.** Then hit return, leaving two spaces between the date and the next text.

◆ **Now type the receiver's contact info on the left side,** aligned below the date. Specifically, type her name, title and mailing address. Above all else, make sure the recipient's name is spelled correctly, and be certain that she is still employed by the organization. Misspelling her name can make or break your chances of employment; and if your letter is sent to someone no longer working for the company, it'll likely hit the trash without anyone ever seeing it.

Hip Tip — *Avoid beginning every sentence with "I." Nothing says "I'm boring" like a dull cover letter. Don't fall into the monotonous trap of including statements such as "I have," "I want," "I do." Being creative (balanced and informative) will help keep your reader from falling asleep.*

◆ **Again, hit return,** and leave two spaces between the receiver's info and the next text.

Hip Tip — *Always proofread a hard copy and, when possible, do not proofread your own work. Since you wrote it, you're more likely to skim over errors. Better yet, get more than one person to proofread your work. This will only increase your chances of having a picture-perfect product.*

◆ **Address your letter with a salutation** like "Dear Ms." or "Dear Mr.," followed by the recipient's last name. (Sticking with "Ms." keeps you in a safe zone that is still acceptable.) If you're replying to a blind ad from the Internet or newspaper and don't have the luxury of a contact name, "Dear Sir or Madam" will suffice.

◆ **Again, hit return** to leave two line spaces between the salutation and the next text.

◆ **Now start the body of your cover letter** by introducing yourself. Good examples are, "I'm currently a senior at Pepperdine University where I'm majoring in psychology," or, "I'm a public relations executive with over seven years of corporate PR experience."

◆ **Tell them why you're writing to them,** and name the exact position you're applying for whenever possible.

◆ **Tell them, in a few sentences, exactly who you are** and what makes you right for the job. (Think of it as if you were trying out speed dating for the first time and you had to impress a hunk.)

Hip Tip   *Check the help wanted ads in your local paper, on the more rep-utable online job boards such as Monster.com, careerbuilder.com, or hotjobs.yahoo.com, or sites specific to an industry, field or company you're interested in working for, like Showbizjobs.com, AmericanAirlines.com, fbi.gov or tamu.edu to better identify the skills and experience employers in your chosen profession are looking for in a potential candidate. Incorporate into your cover letter some key words from their ads — like "resourceful" or "self-starter."*

◆ **Briefly share how you found them.** When possible, use any "ins" you might have, like acquaintances in common or business associations, such as the student division of the American Marketing Association or the leader of the Boys and Girls Club in your area for whom you volunteer.

◆ **Now start a new paragraph** that leads with your background experience that directly relates to the position you're applying for. You can do this by highlighting your qualifications, accomplishments and related job skills, all which should appear on your attached résumé. If you're fresh out of college and have very little internship or real-world experience, spotlight accomplishments, your entrepreneurial spirit, leadership roles and skills. Some to possibly include are your fluency in other languages, artistic awards, treasurer of your sorority and the side jewelry business that you operated in high school, which garnered sales in the thousands.

Hip Tip *Make sure to limit your cover letter to two or three paragraphs, and keep in mind that it is your opportunity to say something your résumé can't, like your desire to relocate to the Midwest or explain your departure from the work force for a year due to your child-rearing responsibilities.*

◆ **Next, cater to their needs.** Tell them that what you bring to the table can help them achieve their goals, and reference the information you've learned about their company or the industry in general.

◆ **The next paragraph** is your chance to take control of your future with the company. Thank the recipient for considering you for the position. Then grab the bull by the horns and tell them that you'll be contacting them. Give a specific day and follow through. (After all, you don't want to pull a boy move. You know what we're talking about — when a guy says he'll call, then he doesn't. Oy!)

◆ **Last, seal the deal.** Complete your letter with a formal closing like "Best regards" or "Sincerely."

Hip Tip *With the fast-paced world of email exchange, chances are a potential employer will ask you to email your résumé. In this case, lose the cover letter as a separate attachment and, instead, cut and paste it into the text of your email. If you're replying to a blind ad via email, use the subject line to reference the special employment code or job title. Otherwise, use the subject line for text that will appeal to the recipient. This will increase your chances of at least getting your email read.*

◆ **Leave four spaces** between the deal-closer and your next text.

◆ **Type your professional name.**

◆ **Finally,** using a black or blue pen, write your autograph in the empty space between the deal-closer and your typed name.

Hip Tip Check out the book WOMEN FOR HIRE: THE ULTIMATE GUIDE TO GETTING A JOB *by Johnson, Spitzman and Pollak. It's a great resource for more detailed examples of well-structured cover letters and résumés and an in-depth compass for the overall job-search process.*

Money Talks

Salary requests can be an immediate way for a human resource team or potential employer to weed people out. Here are the quick and easy steadfast rules for socking it to 'em:

◆ **Don't voluntarily offer up your salary request in writing.** You could quickly alienate your possibilities, or worse, underestimate your worth to an employer and get stuck making a lot less than they were willing to dish over.

◆ **If a company requests your salary history or wage preference,** we suggest you leave it out unless you receive a follow up call or email asking for it.

◆ **If you're asked for a salary history, bullet the last two jobs you've held.** Only list the amount you were making prior to your departure (assuming it was the most you made during your tenure with the company). Factor in the average stipend or commission you make in a year as part of your salary history or annual salary. This way, during the interview process, if they fact check your salary range with your former employer, you can justify why your salary history reflects a much higher figure. However, if you are asked for your BASE salary, don't factor in commission, bonuses or stipends. You'd be outright lying and could talk yourself out of the game entirely.

If a human resource representative reinforces his or her request for your salary expectations, respond with a reasonable range — about

$4,000 to $7,000 — for what is acceptable to you. (Again, this figure should be based on what your research has shown to be a competitive salary and reflect your experience in the field.) For example, if your experience as an office assistant can justify your demand for $42K a year, a figure slightly higher than is typical for the position — we'll say in this case $38K to $40K — you can request a tight range that meets your needs and makes you appear within the employers' league. In this example, request $42K to $45K. If a potential employer really wants you, they'll do their best to get you a salary close to your lowest dollar request and negotiate with other perks. Bottom line: As long as you're reasonable, if there's a will, there's a way. (Keep that in mind, too, when you hear excuses as to why a guy's crazy busy schedule keeps him from arranging a date, despite his persistence in calling.)

◆ **Do not write "negotiable" on your salary request.** (You wouldn't let your husband know in advance that you'd consider cutting him some slack if he made it home from boys' night out later than promised.) If you say it up front, they'll definitely take advantage of it. Don't cut yourself short before even getting started. If you're offering a range for them to consider, then it's a given that you're willing to be a little flexible. Then check out the "Nailing the Negotiations" chapter of this book to successfully negotiate your salary.

Other Staple Accessories that Complete Your Job-Hunt Wardrobe

Whether you're an aspiring make-up artist, Website designer, fashion stylist, public relations professional, teacher, broadcast journalist or still photographer, the best way to sell a potential employer isn't just with your résumé, cover letter or what you say. There are several other tools to show a potential employer how good you are at what you do.

Personal Websites

Given the Internet's quick accessibility to most professionals, developing a Website that spotlights your talent is a great way to prove your ability to an employer before they hire you and to update your contacts about what you've been up to. Streaming videos on the Web can showcase your video wedding scrap-booking business. You can establish even more credibility as a freelance journalist by posting samples of your best published magazine and newspaper articles. Photos truly do speak a thousand words, and your personal Website is a great way to show your art, whether you're an interior designer, painter, photographer or personal fitness trainer. Keep in mind that once you've developed your site, include a link to your "e-cover letter," accompanied by your attached résumé, making it even easier for potential clients or employers to see your genius-ness.

◆ **Letters of recommendation.** Belief in yourself is your best selling tool. But someone else reinforcing your ability is even more reassuring. (I mean, how many of us were inspired to purchase an ab-roller or in-home StairMaster® from testimonials of people like us who said if they could get a body like Cindy Crawford or Jennifer Aniston, so could we?) Now apply that same theory to the work world and impress your potential boss with words of praise from former clients, students, supervisors and colleagues. Are you an elementary school teacher? Consider offering a letter of reference from your principal, a parent or, most importantly, a former student. Are you a waitress looking for your first job as an assistant in corporate America? Why not get a letter of recommendation from your manager and a repeat customer? Showcasing your various professional relationships is a great way to highlight your multiple skills and talents.

Hip Tip   *Don't recommend any reference if you're not absolutely certain they will give you nothing less than a stellar evaluation. And for goodness sakes, ask your reference if it's okay to list them as such, and what contact information you should use (i.e., their cell phone, personal email, etc.). Follow up with them each time you apply for a position if it appears your potential boss might call them to ask about your work ethic. It will allow your reference to tailor his or her comments according to the position and company.*

Portfolios

A portfolio of your finest work is a great way to show off your talent to a potential boss or client. It can also serve as a sample of ideas for a client, like a bride-to-be who's not sure just what kind of flower arrangements she wants at her wedding. If you're a high school or college student trying to get into the creative writing school at New York's prestigious Columbia University, creating a portfolio filled with your best school newspaper stories is a great way to show 'em you've got promise. Include prominent award certificates or visually appealing projects you have successfully implemented in your current position. You can also profile your spectacular letters of recommendation in your portfolio.

Be a Hunter, Not a Sitting Duck

A Hip Girl doesn't stand around waiting for someone to help her put away her luggage in the overhead compartment on a plane. She either asks her neighbor or the flight attendant for assistance or finds a way to lift and store the heavy bag on her own. This is also how a Hip Girl goes about looking for work. Below are some of the best ways to shop ('cause you do it oh so well) for your new job.

Work the Web

◆ **Peruse reputable employment Websites.** They'll tell you what positions are available and where, give a job description, and tell you the skills and experience required to make you a viable candidate. Some will even list the salary range employers are considering.

◆ **Post your résumé on the Web.** Not only can you see what's out there, you can post your résumé on these credible employment Websites. Just like in dating, it's nice when the man steps up and chases after you. Posting your professional Website with a credible employment on-line business broadens your options in a target-rich environment and lets an employer court you.

Hip Tip *To find a Website that posts job listings in your area, log onto the Internet and type in your city, state and the words "job listings." EXAMPLE: San Francisco, CA, & job listings. Also, post your résumé on job board sites for human resources representatives to see. Oftentimes, human resource reps will pay a subscription to browse through online job board résumés. Make sure to use key industry words of skill or certification in your résumé that, in a broad search by an HR representative, will automatically make your résumé pop up.*

◆ **Stalk your industry-specific employment sites or your favorite company's Website.** You know what you want, and we say, right on! The only one holding you back is you. To find industry-specific employment sites, check out national or local bureaus of related associations or organizations. For instance, if you want a teaching job in California, contact the local district offices in the various cities you want to work in. Keep in mind that not all districts, companies or fields are computer savvy or up to date, nor do they post job openings on their Websites. So contacting the personnel department is also important.

◆ **Enlist a headhunter.** Job-hunting is time-consuming and somewhat costly. So consider maximizing your efforts by enlisting a professional in your field to help. Once you've passed their qualifications and impressed them as professional, headhunters and placement agencies — from entry level to executive search firms — actively search and arrange job interviews for you for free, banking on your employment potential. (Heads up: Don't let anyone charge you a fee. It could be a scam.) Headhunters and placement agencies get their money not from you, but from legitimate companies who hire them to find impressive, qualified candidates. (Most placement agencies specialize in temporary placement services, which can also be a great way to get your foot in the door. See more on that below.) Ah, but there is a price in this deal: Placement agencies will find many candidates to offer their client in the hopes one will stick and therefore make them some cash. (Think of it like the "numbers" approach to dating: Go out with enough men and hope one of them will be worth marrying.) And remember, they are your representative to your future. Be selective when selecting your "face" person(s). Ask questions like their success ratio for placing candidates, their client list and history. Unless you've agreed to exclusivity, you can enlist more than one agency. And most important, don't surrender your future entirely to them. Ultimately, you are responsible for paying your rent, so keep your eye out for opportunities as well.

HipTip *To find a headhunter or placement agency in your area, check out your local yellow pages under "employment agencies." Also, look for industry-specific agencies on the Web using your industry as a key word, paired with "employment agencies."*

In-house and Out-source Temporary Pools

In-house and out-source temporary agencies work to put you in schools of people on whom they rely when they quickly need a short-term job role filled (like when you were younger and your full-time teacher got sick so they called in a substitute). Many human resources departments and various administrations interview candidates for their company in-house temporary pools to call on in an emergency. Earning a coveted in-house temporary pool position is a great way to learn more about the company and field in which you're interested. It's also a great way to discover exactly what department of an industry best suits you without investing too many years. Meanwhile, you're getting paid for it.

Go Career Shopping at the Fair

No, not the fair with funnel cakes and a Ferris wheel. Explore new career options or break into the work force at community career fairs. It's a great way to make initial connections with professionals in your fields of interest. (See the networking section below for more.) But at the end of the day, if nothing captures your attention, at least you'll have gained invaluable interviewing and networking experience.

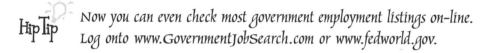

Hip Tip   *To find career fairs in your area, check with your local employment office or in the employment section of your local newspaper. Larger cities post career fair opportunities at sites like craigslist.com. For national postings, check out www.careerfairs.com. Also, many local Chamber of Commerce offices offer upcoming job fairs or business expos in your area. Business fairs act as another great source to network with people who work in the field you do.*

Your Good Old-fashioned State Employment Offices

Like using a pen and pad to write a letter, or drinking your coffee straight up instead of ordering a trendy latte, the regular ol' employment office still exists to post a multitude of open positions for unemployed people. True, you'll have to dig through a plethora of jobs that may not appeal to you, and depending on your level of experience, you may or may not find something that will utilize all your talents. But if you're a full-time student looking for a summer gig, or a full-time mom looking for part-time administrative work to keep your social skills afloat, your local employment agency might be worth a stop-by to see if there's something that sparks your interest.

Hip Tip   *Now you can even check most government employment listings on-line. Log onto www.GovernmentJobSearch.com or www.fedworld.gov.*

Net-WORK the System

The word "work" isn't part of the word "network" without reason. Going out and creating opportunities to be seen and heard isn't all that easy. (Similarly, curling up to read a book at home every night after a full day of working doesn't make meeting new friends or a possible love connection very likely.) You've got to muster up the energy and courage to actively find people who can help you achieve your professional goals. And remember, getting out alone will not snag you a job opportunity. Just like in dating, where you've got to get your flirt on through smiling, eye contact and conversation, you've also got to work your charm in professional networking situations. After all, first impressions are everlasting. A couple of easy ways to network are listed below.

◆ **Internships.** Internships are a means of getting short-term experience in a line of work you're interested in while building relationships with people who can help you. Some internships are paid, while many others are for school-credit only. In exchange for the experience, a company gets your laborious efforts. Treat internships as if they were jobs, maintaining your professionalism at all times. Start as early as your college freshman year, or even high school if you can. Try as many in the different areas of the field you're interested in. For example, if you're interested in journalism, take internships in television news, newspapers, radio stations, magazines and public relations offices. It'll help you figure out your niche quicker in a broad field. And remember, internships teach you both what you do and don't want to do for a future career. So no experience is a wasted one. Last, but equally important to note, internships can work in your favor as a means for switching career fields. Businesses value experience and ambition. If you show them you're willing to work for little or no money to gain experience, that speaks volumes to a potential employer.

Hip Tip *The best way to locate internships are through your college's department head or career office, by calling the companies or organizations you'd really like to work for (try both the human resources department and the department you're interested in), or online intern-listing resources like intern-web.com, wetfeet.com or monstertrak.monster.com*

◆ **Join professional organizations, clubs and associations.** Belonging to your local chapter of the Parent/Teacher Association (PTA), Junior League or the student version of the Public Relations Society of America (PSA) puts you in the mix with people who are like you and can help you climb your career ladder.

Hip Tip *To enlist help from other Hip Girls like you who might be in a position to help you get a leg up in the profession of your choice, contact the Business Women's Network at www.bwni.com or 202/466-8209. It's the largest directory for contact information of women's organizations around the world. National Association of Female Executives (NAFE) is another organization devised for us professional gals to get ahead. Contact them at www.NAFE.com or 800/927-6233. For a complete list of links to a multitude of other career women organizations to help you network, check out www.womensbusinessresearch.org/links.html.*

◆ **Target specific companies or offices.** If you know what you want and who you want to work for — like as a pilot for United Airlines because you hear they offer the best benefits package or as a police officer in lower-income areas because you want to make a difference to underprivileged boys and girls — specifically and persistently target your job inquiries with those companies and regions. This method is typically slower in finding a job, as it usually requires a position to open up. But if you've got the will, patience, follow-through and drive, most employers will recognize that over time. So while you may have to take another job in the meantime, you can still realize your dream.

Hip Tip *When targeting specific companies or offices, don't rely solely on the human resources department. If you know what department you want* to work for, attempt to contact and network with someone in the department who can help you get your foot in the door. Ultimately, they may send you back to the human resources department for procedural purposes, but at least you will have taken as much charge as possible of your future. See the "You Talkin' to Me?" chapter for more tips on making cold calls for networking purposes.

◆ **Volunteer.** Whether you volunteer at your local animal shelter or are a "Big Sister" to a little girl in need of your positive influence through the YMCA's Ypal program, you never know what new passions you might discover and where your next career opportunities might come from. The point is, get out and do something that makes you feel good, gives back to your community, and, perhaps, albeit an unintentional but pleasant benefit, will get a lead to your next job opportunity.

◆ **That's what friends (and family) are for.** Put the word out to the people who know and love you the most. If they can support your quest for career happiness, we're sure they will.

—⊰⊱—

Job-hunting is rarely fun. But diligent and persistent execution up front can create a plethora of unforeseen opportunities for you to choose from. Stay focused and determined, and don't waiver by rejection. Some of life's biggest successes were preceded by numerous misadventures.

The Audition:

Tips for Your Best Interview Performance

"I was so psyched when I got an interview for an internship with a famous celebrity stylist. I stressed for days about what outfit was fashion forward enough for the interview. So when the stylist answered the door with nothing but boxer briefs on, I was mortified! I wanted to turn and run. But somehow, I made it through the entire interview with a straight face and got the internship. It was proof that if I could get through that incredibly awkward situation, I could survive anything the internship threw at me."

—Lilah, 23, Full-time Student/Intern

You only get one chance to make a good first impression. Only preparation will ensure a better chance of a successful interview process. There's a plethora of things you need to do before sitting across the desk from your potential employer: Select the right outfit; pack your briefcase with your résumé and portfolio materials; research the company, industry and competition; and print directions to ensure your prompt arrival. However, nothing is more critical than tailoring your answers and questions for your interview. Put yourself in your potential employer's shoes and ask yourself what that person might want to know, then role play with a friend. To help you achieve your best, we're listing some of the most common questions employers ask. Keep in mind, they may not ask them exactly as we've written them, but the underlying questions will be similar (just like men who use an assortment of pick-up lines for the same intention of getting your digits).

◆ **What is your work style?** Your work style can encompass any trait from multi-tasker to team player, or detailed-oriented to big-picture thinker. Only you truly know you. Be honest with what you prefer, but note that being flexible is one of your biggest selling tools for working with people whose various work styles might be different from yours. (See the "Colleague Camaraderie" chapter for more.)

HipTip *Speaking of style, dress appropriately for your interview. If you don't have a suit, or you're not sure if it's necessary to wear one, do some investigating. You can call the human resources department of the company and inquire about the company's dress code. Better yet, take a field trip to the place where you'll be interviewing at lunchtime. Take note how employees are dressed. Overall, it's better to "overdress" for the interview than to dress too casually.*

◆ **Do you prefer to work as a team or independently?** Ask yourself what the position you're interviewing for tends to require. Be honest with yourself and your potential boss. If you definitely prefer one style over the other, it's okay to say so . . . and you should (otherwise you risk looking like you're giving the ever-politically correct beauty queen reply). However, follow it up with a couple of examples that show your versatility, like when you had to work with the other fifth grade teachers to plan and execute the field trip. Or spotlight your independent work abilities. Explain how you consistently surpassed your sales quotas in your pharmaceutical sales job even though you had to work independently and be self-disciplined since there was no set work schedule or supervisor managing your day-to-day efforts.

Hip Tip *Hop on to your computer and surf the Net. Do as much research as you can about the business where you are interviewing before the big day arrives. Knowing as much as you can about the company's products, lingo, customers, services and competitors will give you an edge. Once you have a firm grasp on what the company does and its general mission, all that's left to do is show them how well you'll fit their needs.*

◆ **Tell me more about your responsibilities at your last job.** Be concise by summing up your responsibilities in categories that show skills like customer service, management or leadership roles, budgetary and organizational responsibilities, and so on. But be sure to follow each category of responsibility with specific examples that highlight your success. For instance, did you manage all elements of the company's special events including a staff of over 100, vendors, clients and the $700,000 budget? It's these kinds of details that will set you apart from the rest.

Hip Tip *It's important to explain recent, long-term gaps in work. If your last job was a year ago because you left the work force to be a stay-at-home mom, or you saved up the funds to take a year off and travel, offer short but direct explanations. Close your explanation with how your time off helped develop other skills applicable to the position you're applying for. More difficult time-off occurrences to explain, like rehabilitation from drugs and* alcohol, mental stress or treating a lingering medical ailment can be camouflaged as "travel," "taking care of an ill parent" or "an imminent family problem." Just make sure to reinforce that the problem has been resolved and won't affect your employment.

◆ **What are your strengths?** Keep them relative to the job you're applying for. Now's not the time to talk about your ability to throw a cute outfit together unless you're working in the fashion and beauty industry. Cite skills the position requires. Also, don't give generic, cliché answers such as you're a real people person. But if you feel that's true, say something like, "I get along well with all kinds of people because I'm a good listener and can read people's needs quickly."

◆ **What are areas you can improve on?** It's important to be honest with your interviewer. A good interviewer will know a line of bull when she sees it. Turn your negative into a positive for the company. For instance, "I have high standards and get impatient with results that show less than someone's best," or, "I'm a decision maker and often get impatient with people who spend too much time questioning what to do."

Tip Tip *If you're asked a question you don't understand, ask for further clarification. Asking an interviewer to restate a question isn't awful, but giving a completely off-the-topic response can be detrimental.*

◆ **What do you see in your near future?** Again, your employer cares about your professional life. So don't necessarily volunteer that you and your husband want to start a family in the next year. Instead, focus on your interest in growing with a solid company, taking on more responsibility, or, at the very least, learning more about the industry.

Hip Tip *Exact laws on questions pertaining to your personal life vary from state to state. Generally speaking, it's illegal for a potential employer to inquire about information related to marital status, age, race, religion, national origin, physical disabilities, physical appearance or sex. Pregnancy, whether you're in the middle of a term or have plans to start a family, is protected by law, but it is within an interviewer's rights to ask an applicant if she can perform the essential functions of the job with reasonable accommodation.*

◆ **Describe a conflict in your last job and how you resolved it.** Talk about how your approach successfully alleviated the problem. Don't be negative and dwell on or fault your difficult boss, colleague or client. Craft your answer so that you look like you were part of the solution and express how much that experience taught you.

◆ **What is the success you're most proud of from your last job?** Don't just say what it was. Give a concise example of how and why it was your proudest moment. Why not share two? Hey, when you're good, you're good.

◆ **If I were to ask your boss, client or colleague about your style, what would they say?** No matter your experience — good or bad — make sure your answer reflects the positive opportunities you gained from your last place of employment. Even a challenging experience presents an opportunity for growth. It's important to be mindful of your downfalls, but spin them in a way that makes you look good. For example, "My former boss taught me a lot about this profession and my work style. I think she'd say I'm dedicated, respectful of others and encourage their opinions, and that I've really grown into a strong and confident manager of people."

Hip Tip   *An interviewer may ask to contact current and former employers as references to your work performance. If you're currently employed and don't want your employer to know you're looking for another job, it's okay to tell the interviewer not to contact the employer since he or she doesn't know you're looking for a new job. But, if you have a copy of a recent review from your supervisor that clearly shows you're nothing less than stellar, consider showing it to your potential employer. You should offer up other former supervisors as references who can talk candidly and positively about your work efforts. Make sure, however, to offer references who have agreed to it, and notify them whenever they may hear from a potential employer.*

◆ **What's your management style?** Make sure to express that you openly communicate with your employees, clearly set expectations, but invite and encourage them to share their questions, ideas and opinions with you. Offer examples from your previous management experience to illustrate your point.

◆ **Tell me why you left your last job.** The best answer, in particular if you're coming from a bad situation, is that there was limited opportunity for growth. Other plausible reasons for changing your job are relocation or work schedule accommodations. Do not say you hated the new management or that you didn't get the time off you had requested.

Hip Tip   *Explaining a layoff or firing situation can be challenging. Attribute your layoff to a flagging economy or an overall corporate downsizing. In case you were fired, no matter what the reason, position it as if you left the job to explore other opportunities, industries or lines of business. Most former employers will avoid dishing the dirt on you because it could make them vulnerable to a lawsuit. Therefore, many larger HR teams adopt a policy of not providing references. But, because we're all human after all, it's safer to prepare for* a loose cannon. Therefore, check with your former employer's HR department regarding their policy about references. In smaller companies, contact your former boss and ask what kinds of things would be said if you offered him or her as a reference. (Don't list a peer as a reference as this sends an automatic red flag to potential employers of a hostile work relationship.) If you know there's potential for a bad reference from a former employer, arm yourself with the information you need to create a smart, yet honest, defense. If you're certain a potential employer will contact a former, hostile employer, delicately explain the circumstances. Employers don't like surprises. Do damage control before the damage is done and keep yourself in the running. Again, avoid placing blame on others or fault-finding with the company. Calling your old boss "psycho" isn't going to set well.

◆ **Why do you want to work for this company or why do you want this position?** Why do you? Do you know? Here's a chance to show you did your homework about them and the industry, and that you have a clear goal for your future.

◆ **We'd like to take you to the next step,** which is doing some assessment tests and a background check. Before we do, is there anything we should be aware of? Yikes! This is tricky, for sure. You might be sitting there thinking, "Will that cold medicine or your rare, late-night drinking session register as something worse?" Or perhaps you made a foolish mistake on your 21st birthday and got a Driving Under the Influence ticket. While it's illegal in many states to request this information on an application, it may not be illegal in your state to ask it in an interview. If this concerns you, know your state's rules. Also, know what your records say about you. Many records are open to the public for review, depending on federal and state-by-state laws. (Just ask Wynona Ryder, whose five-fingered-discount shopping indiscretion was open for all the world to scrutinize.) Some such documents that might affect you include government contracts with businesses; birth, marriage and death records; court files; arrest records; property ownership and tax information; minutes of meetings of government entities; driver's license information; occupational licenses; and Securities and Exchange Commission filings. You should also request a copy of your credit report before beginning your job hunt, especially if you're concerned you may have skeletons in your closet to explain to a potential employer. (See the "Stolen Identity" chapter of *The Hip Girl's Handbook for Home, Car & Money Stuff* for information on ordering a copy of your credit report.) Clean up and remove what you can from all your records prior to applying for job openings. This is especially important if you have bad credit, which can adversely affect your chances for retail positions. As for drug consumption, take your prescribed medication with you to the drug test so there is no confusion. Also, if you have reason to be concerned, get tested at a certified clinic before submitting your application for a job. (Those home kits aren't reliable.) Look up "drug clinics" in the yellow pages of your local phone book. A general drug test costs about $30. But if, after all your preparation, you're still faced with such a dilemma, the best way to reply to a potentially damaging question is to tell the truth, noting it was a unique situation and that it won't happen in the future.

HipTip *Many employers require you to take tests as part of their hiring process. Don't be offended; it's often a requirement for everyone at many different levels. Some of these might test your written skills; others are based on psychological evaluations or career ambitions. Be honest on multiple-choice questions. Employers may question your character if you respond that you'd rather work for yourself than answer to a boss. Embrace the opportunity to learn something about yourself. Use this as an opportunity to navigate* whether or not the position you're applying for will maximize your assets. (Read more in the "Working Your Assets" chapter.)

◆ **How much do you want to make?** Check out the "Money Talks" section in "The Basics" or read "Nailing the Negotiations" chapters for more. Avoid offering an amount that takes you out of the running, or worse, puts you in a position to earn less than you could have negotiated.

Hip Tip *Nothing could be more annoying than a phone ringing during your interview. Before entering the office building, make sure that your cell phone is off.*

What Do You Want to Know?

Remember that you're interested in making a career for yourself. Finding the right fit — at least for now — is important so you can build a structure to grow from. Therefore, interview back by asking some select questions that help you decide whether the position and the work environment is suitable to you. (Just make sure to come across inquisitively. Don't take too much of an "I might be too good for you" attitude. Employers might be put off by your arrogance.) Some questions to come to the table with include:

◆ **How did this position become available?** Did someone leave or is the department expanding?

◆ **Is there training involved,** and if so, what kind?

◆ **What traits or work style do you prefer** from someone in this role?

◆ **What are some of the upcoming challenges** the person in this position will be tackling?

◆ **What's your timeframe for hiring someone to fill this position?** When might I expect to hear from you? Do you mind if I call you in a couple of weeks to check in about the status of your decision?

◆ **What are the department's or company's growth plans?**

◆ **What other abilities do you frequently need** from the person filling this position, like the ability to travel at the last minute or work overtime or on weekends?

◆ **Do you have any questions or concerns that I can clear up for you?** (This question should be used as a closer and serves as your chance to clarify any responses that may not have set well with the employer.)

HipTip *Your first interview isn't necessarily the right time to address questions about paid vacations and holidays or whether your benefits package is impressive. Leave those questions for either the Human Resources rep or for your second and third interviews. Remember, your first interview is to get them excited about you and to gauge if you're interested in the position.*

Follow Through with Follow Up

Like building any kind of relationship, whether personal, romantic or professional, you will want to follow up with your new contact to show your interest.

◆ **Send a handwritten thank-you note,** regardless if you think you got the job or not. Send it within 24 hours of your interview so that you're still top of mind to the employer. Thank them for their time, and find something specific to mention that struck your fancy — like a mutual acquaintance, a specific responsibility of the job or something you discovered you share in common with the interviewer. Reiterate your interest in the position. Then close with your personal contact information. This makes it especially important to always ask the person who interviews you for a business card. It will serve as a good record of your search and help ensure correct information (i.e., spelling of name and title) for sending the thank-you letter.

Hip Tip   *Email thank-you notes are becoming increasingly acceptable for fast-paced, high-travel industries. So if your potential employer is rarely in the office or you noticed that his mail was stacked to the ceiling, emailing your note will suffice. Follow the same guidelines for the contents of a hand-written note and check out the "You Talkin' to Me?" chapter for email etiquette.*

◆ **Follow through with a phone call commitment.** Just like you expect your girlfriend to call to firm up tentative plans, do the same with a potential boss. If you closed the interview with a request to make a follow-up call the following week about the status of the position, and the potential employer was amicable to it, do it. And be timely with your call. Keeping top of mind with a potential employer and showing follow through on a promise will speak volumes about your interest in the position and your work ethic. Follow the "You Talkin' to Me?" chapter's suggestions on work phone etiquette.

◆ **Keep your chin up.** If you find out you didn't get this job, trust that your efforts will pay off on a job more fitting for your expertise and ambitions. Just like in finding Mr. Right, where break-ups and reunions happen for a reason, not getting a job might be a blessing in disguise for your future opportunities. Truly.

◆ **Maintain your new contact.** Just because this position wasn't right for you, or another candidate narrowly beat you out of the job due to more experience, update your new contact semi-regularly with the new experience you've gained in the related industry. Email or snail mail your latest résumé, cover letter and portfolio. Also request they keep you in mind for similar positions that you might be qualified for, and ask if you may check in with them every so often.

Interviewing for a new job is both exciting and nerve racking. But like making a new recipe for a dinner party, preparation and practice are the keys to succeeding.

Human Resources Breakdown:

It's to Your "Benefit"

"It was my first year of teaching, and I'd gone out the night before paint-ing the town red. I woke up sick as a puppy the next morning after con-suming one too many sake bombs. I couldn't call in sick because I didn't have lesson plans completed for the day. So I pulled myself together as best I could. It was only a matter of a couple of hours before one of the stu-dents announced, 'You're turning green!' and I slyly vomited in the trash-can beside my desk. Luckily, none of the students noticed my little indis-cretion, and the principal was able to secure a mid-day substitute for me. No one ever found out that my "flu" bug was actually self-inflicted. To this day, I have sworn off any late weeknight partying!"

—Melissa, 29, Elementary School Teacher

"Get a good job with decent pay and good benefits." Ever hear that from your mom and dad? Probably only since you started your first paper route gig at the tender age of twelve. Back then, and maybe even still today, you were looking at your dad wondering what in the world he was talking about. Fortunately, we're here to spell out the basics for you because we know that all that health insurance and stock options, maternity leave and 'fully vested' lingo is practically a foreign language. But just like going to a dreadful gynecology appointment for a yearly check-up is important to your health, so too is reading this chapter's information, no matter how lackluster the subject matter is. You'll thank us for it, trust us.

Insurance Coverage

Getting your health or life protected (and how well) is one of the biggest, most important benefits for you to consider when deciding whether to take a position, even if it comes with a little less pay.

Medical Insurance

This is the insurance that covers your everyday well-being. America has several health insurance coverage plans. Each state and organizational plan varies. Check with the employer to see what is specifically offered and required. Below are some of the more standard forms. But before we explain them, keep in mind that a company may require you to work for them for a certain amount of time before benefits kick in, or that you pay for a portion of your premium coverage. For some companies, your health insurance benefits will start from Day One of your employment. Others may require a waiting period for typically 30, 60 or 90 days before you earn your medical coverage benefit.

◆ **Health Maintenance Organization (HMO)** is a health plan that involves how your health care is delivered, meaning through HMO-only managed facilities, doctors, pharmacies and health plans. Like finding a good mechanic, we recommend you consult a few doctors in the HMO system before deciding on the one that best fits your needs. Now, here's the simplified version of HMO insurance coverage pros and cons:

HMO PROS:

□   It's usually more affordable than other forms of insurance plans.

□   It's usually one-stop shopping because all your medical, vision and pharmacy needs are housed at each full-service facility.

□   Co-payments (the money you pay at the time of your visit, which can run anywhere from $10 to $15 or more) tend to be less expensive.

HMO CONS:

□   You're only allowed to select a physician from the choices that the HMO offers.

□   HMOs often feel less personal with a more "get 'em in and get 'em out" type of customer service.

□   You must first get permission from your primary care doctor if you need to see a specialist.

□   You can only get the kind of treatment or procedure the HMO offers. So if a new, less invasive surgical procedure isn't yet practiced by your HMO, you'll get the old-school method.

☐ You must go to your HMO facility as long as one is within a pre-specified distance from you. Even in the case of an emergency, if there's a hospital nearby that's not part of your HMO, you must go the extra distance to get to your HMO facility.

◆ **Preferred Provider Organization or Option (PPO)** is a health plan that gives you more control of the delivery of your services. This type of insurance encourages you to see "in-network" doctors (a collection of pre-selected, independently housed physicians who you can choose from for your medical needs) or allows you to choose "out-of-network" doctors (physicians not on the PPO's pre-selected list). But with this more flexible plan comes varying coverages. The bottom line: Know exactly what your plan says. Here are the general pros and cons of a PPO.

PPO PROS:

☐ PPO "in-house" co-payments are reasonable (usually around $10 to $20) as long as you stay within the group's pre-selected network of doctors.

☐ You can see any "in-network" doctor, including specialists like dermatologists or orthopedic surgeons, without seeing a primary care physician first.

☐ Your PPO coverage typically pays for all or most all of your "in-network" medical services (for example, they pay 80 percent and you pay 20 percent).

☐ Your PPO will cover a pre-determined percent to see a doctor outside the network (but not without paying a "penalty" of sorts if that same service is offered by an "in-house" doctor).

PPO CONS:

☐ Your co-pay is usually more expensive than that of an HMO.

□   If you decide to see a physician who is not on the "in-network" physicians' list, you will likely be required to pay a pre-set deductible before getting your medical expenses covered (deductibles typically run between $250 and $1,000 or more), or pay the difference between what the "in-network" doctors charge vs. what the "out-of-network" doctors charge for the same procedure.

□   If you see a doctor out of the network, you may have to pay the bill out of your own pocket first. Then you can submit it for reimbursement on your own. *Yikes!*

□   Your pre-set coverage percentage for a doc who is not part of the PPO network will probably be less. For instance, your PPO may only pay 70 percent (or less) of the bill for a doc not on their "network" list. Yep, that means it's up to you to pay for the other 30 percent.

◆   **Point of Service (POS).** POS is managed care which offers a pre-selected pool of physicians who belong to a network with a deductible (like in a PPO) and co-pay (usually around $10 to $20) that must first be met. Here's the dealio:

POS PROS:

□   They are more flexible than HMOs.

□   You may visit a doctor outside the network and still receive some insurance coverage.

□   If your "in-network" doctors don't offer the newest procedure you read about in *Cosmo* for, say, acne control, you can see an "out-of-network" physician who does. (Just make sure your plan covers treatment for your ailment first.)

POS CONS:

□   They are not as liberal as a PPO.

□ A POS requires you to select and see a primary care physician prior to seeing a specialist.

□ If you visit a specialist without getting a referral first, you're responsible for submitting the bill to your insurance provider for reimbursement. Sometimes, the follow-through and follow-up is a bit of a hassle; it can be time consuming and frustrating.

□ The portion your POS insurance will pay for your "out-of-network" doctor visit is substantially less than what it would pay for an "in-network" doctor visit. And guess who pays for those overages? Yep! You, baby!

Hip Tip *Some larger organizations, which consistently employ large numbers of full-time freelance and temporary employees, offer special health insurance and retirement plans. These special plans often require a permanent freelancer to meet certain standards before qualifying for such benefits, generally including working full time and consecutively for six months to a year or more. Inquire with your human resources department for the specifics of your organization's policy on this matter.*

Prescription Drug Coverage

For a relatively nominal co-payment fee (anywhere from $5 to $25 or more at each pharmacy visit), your insurance may cover your prescription fees. Whooeeee! That may even mean "the pill," for as long as your insurance covers it. And in today's technologically advanced world, on-line purchasing or regular mail ordering can keep you from having to stand in line at your local pharmacy.

Benefits packages come in all different shapes and sizes, depending on the company size, industry and geographic location. But, according to the U.S. Chamber of Commerce 2003 survey, a healthy benefits packet can add an average of $16,617 per employee. So, when negotiating your salary, don't forget your human resources department is factoring in your overall cost to them.

Dental Assistance Insurance

We've said it before and we'll reinforce it once more: Your smile is one of your best workplace accessories. To keep teeth pearly white and healthy, it's best if you get your workplace to cover all or most of your dental insurance coverage. But just like in medical insurance coverage, a company may require that you work for them for a designated amount of time before you're covered. A couple of different, standard options include:

◆ **Preferred Provider Organization (PPO) for Dental Insurance.** It operates similarly to a PPO in the medical insurance business.

◆ **Dental Maintenance Organization (DMO)** or Dental HMO Plan. It operates similarly to an HMO in the medical insurance business.

According to the book HUMAN RESOURCES by Barron's Business Library, The Health Insurance Portability and Accountability Act of 1996 gives additional protection to all workers, including employees, self-employed, small businesses and uninsured people with preexisting health conditions. The provisions of the Act guarantee that a person currently covered by health insurance through an employer can switch jobs without fear of losing coverage even if she or a family member suffers from a preexisting chronic illness (as long as a new job is started within one year of her departure from her old job). The Act also prohibits group insur-

ance plans from dropping coverage for a sick employee (or her employer), sets up tax-deductible medical savings accounts for small businesses, self-employed and the uninsured, and increases tax deductibility for premiums of self-employed people from 30 percent to 80 percent by the year 2006.

Vision Insurance

This insurance covers the exorbitant costs of eyeglasses, contact lenses, check-ups and other eye-related issues. This can be expensive if you have to pay for it on your own. Check with your company for what they offer. If they don't offer this coverage, try to negotiate it into your contract.

Flexible Spending Accounts (FSA)

A Flexible Spending Account enables your company to automatically deduct a tax-free, predetermined amount of money set by you from each paycheck into a fund that you can use to offset various insurance premiums, non-reimbursable medical or dental expenses, or the cost of child and dependent care costs. There is usually a limit to the total annual amount deposited in the account, dependent on your company's policy. At the beginning of each plan year, you, the employee, can estimate and pay for such out-of-pocket expenses for the year. Then, at the end of the year, you submit your claims to your employer who then issues a tax-free check. Both the employer and employee benefit from this pre-tax system, since no Social Security, federal income tax, or state and local taxes are deducted from the reimbursed amount. What's the catch? The Internal Revenue System (IRS), you know, Uncle Sam, has a "use it or lose it" policy. Therefore, any money left over in the account goes bye-bye. It can't be rolled over to the next year or refunded in anyway.

Hip Tip *The annual salary you negotiate is called gross pay. Don't be alarmed when your paycheck is substantially less than what you'd expected due to bizarre automatic deductions you may or may not have authorized. This would be your take-home pay, otherwise called net income. Many of the deductions from your net income are courtesy of Uncle Sam. (You know, you remember him from the Taxes section of THE HIP GIRL'S HANDBOOK FOR HOME, CAR & MONEY STUFF.) So expect to see several tax deductions, usually federal and state taxes and, perhaps, some local taxes as well. There are also often a couple of Federal Insurance Contribution Act (FICA) charges, including one that goes toward Medicare — for when you retire and need government health care assistance — and Old-Age Survivors and Disability Insurance (OASDI), which is the official name for Social Security. Any medical and dental insurance premiums will most likely be withdrawn automatically by your employer. Some states may deduct a state disability tax if your company doesn't cover it. And don't forget, the deductions you opted for, including your FSA and any retirement or educational contributions you may have allocated, like your 401(k) or 403 (b) or 529 college fund.*

Basic Life Insurance

Basic life insurance offers financial protection to your family in case you die. It may also extend, with limitations, to your husband and kids. Most companies base an employee's basic life insurance coverage on anywhere from one to three times an employee's base salary. If you're lucky, your company will pay for 100 percent of your total premium costs. Otherwise, perhaps you should negotiate it.

Accidental Death and Dismemberment Insurance (ADDI)

We hate to sound morbid, but in the terrible event you die or lose a limb or eye, you will want to make sure you and your family have an income to survive on, especially if the injury prevents you from working again. This is what ADDI is for. A company pays for all or a portion of an employee's ADDI coverage in the event of an injury caused directly and exclusively by external, violent and purely accidental means. The amount an employee is awarded is based on her annual base salary (typically either half, equal to or two to three times her salary base). Sorry, but nope. You can't factor in that fat bonus or commission check you worked so hard to make. And there is a predetermined maximum amount — like $3 million (which we all know doesn't go as far as it used to; just ask all the television reality show winners).

Worker's Compensation Insurance

Worker's compensation insurance covers employees who incur injuries as a result of an accident on the job, and in some cases, even if the employee goofs off and breaks a leg during working hours. This insurance coverage is especially important if you work in an environment that requires operating heavy equipment, working with hazardous chemicals or working in a high-risk job, such as firefighter, flight attendant or pilot. This is an employer-paid insurance as mandated by the federal government. With it comes paid time off while you recuperate. But, as with most situations, there are loopholes. Consult your HR representative or an attorney if necessary.

Hip Tip *Currently, five states have their own state-funded worker's compensation to which employers are required to contribute. These are Washington, Wyoming, North Dakota, West Virginia and Ohio. Meanwhile, some employers are self-insured, meaning they pay their own claims but are still regulated by the state, while some employers use insurance agencies.*

Business Travel Insurance

If you travel for your job, whether by train, plane or automobile, and you get hurt or, heaven forbid, die while on the road on business, you or your benefactor are entitled to the money your business travel insurance plan pays out. Again, this amount is determined by your company's policy and is typically several times the amount of your annual salary base, but can only be as much as their pre-set specified amount. Most businesses that require frequent travel pay 100 percent of your premium charges.

Short-term or Long-term Disability Plans

In the event you should need to take time off from work due to an injury that prevents you from temporarily performing your job, a company's short-term or long-term disability plan can help you offset your loss of wages during unpaid time off. An excellent coverage plan will have your company paying 100 percent of the plan's annual premium. How long and how much of your salary is covered during your leave varies from company to company. For instance, one company might pay 100 percent of your salary for the first six weeks, and then decrease their payment to 80 percent for the next three months, and so on. And of course the plan usually has a pre-set limit.

Tip Tip *Some states automatically withdraw a percentage from your paycheck to put toward State Disability. (Not all do, so find out if your state does.) If so, you can file for disability reimbursement through your state, which can help you alleviate the loss of wages due to an injury. However, if your company has its own short- and long-term disability plan, from which you are probably receiving more money, your company may ask you to give them your state disability check to help them alleviate some of their costs for covering your disability pay. To find out more about filing for disability in your state, punch in the key words "employ-ment" or "workforce," then "development department" and your state.*

Long-term Care (LTC) Plans

Long-term care provides assistance to an employee who needs extended care due to an illness, accident or age. Coverage is for either in-home care or a stay in a long-term care facility. Some companies offer to pay the entire LTC premiums for upper management and exec-utives, while others pay for a portion for middle- to low-level manage-ment. Other companies offer discounted premiums, but require the employee to pay for it in full, and this usually costs a pretty penny. Meanwhile, many other businesses don't even offer LTC coverage. Note that some LTC coverage can be extended to specified family members. Check with your company about their policy.

Employee-paid Insurance Options

Insurance companies sometimes offer a discounted mass rate to a company's employees for insurance coverage that generally falls to employees to pay. Such plans might include personal accident insur-ance and supplemental life insurance for yourself, your husband or your dependent children.

◆ **Personal accident insurance.** An employee may purchase indi-vidual or family coverage up to a specified, predetermined amount, which can be above and beyond the coverage that the employer already pays for an employee who is accidentally injured and cannot work.

◆ **Supplemental life insurance.** An employee may purchase addi-tional life insurance coverage above and beyond what an employer pays in the case of the employee's death. Typically speaking, an employee can purchase several times her base salary (maxing out at a pre-set figure, of course) for her partner and for each dependent child until he or she reaches a specified age, usually age twenty-three.

Hip Tip *Purchasing supplemental life insurance for yourself, your partner or your kids requires each candidate to meet the Evidence of Insurability (EOI) standards enforced by the insurance provider. Inquire with HR or your insurance provider to determine the specific requirements.*

Money, Money, Money

We highly recommend that you go after your heart's passion to make your living. However, we aren't naive enough to think you can survive on love of your job alone. (By the way, neither can a marriage. Sorry, ladies, we aren't here to perpetuate the romanticized Hollywood love story. We're real girls helping our sisters navigate through the realities of life.) Let's face it, whether you love your job or hate it, money does serve as a motivating factor to some degree. So let's go over some of the money-related benefits you should consider when determining to stick with your current job or switch to another.

Retirement Plans

There are several retirement plans. The one you choose depends on what kind of organization or position you're applying for — like for the government or state, or with a non-profit company or as a Hip Girl heading up your very own business.

◆ **401(k).** This is the retirement plan that most for-profit companies offer. It allows you to deduct money from each paycheck before the government gets its hands on it, depending, of course, on what your company's plan offers. As of 2005, the government allows you to contribute a maximum of $14,000 to this fund annually.

Hip Tip — *Some companies offer a matching program as an incentive for their employees to save for their future by deferring taxes on wages and earned income. (Girl, a free ride stopped the day your parents required you to do chores for $5 a week. A company matching program might be the closest thing you ever experience to free money, so you'd better take advantage of it.) In this program, a company will match an employee's contributions to her retirement account using a pre-defined formula. For example, a company might determine its match based on its performance in the market that year and a pre-determined percentage (let's say 50 percent) of your portion (let's say 5 percent) of your pre-tax contributions. For example:*

Annual Salary	$ 40,000.00	$ 50,000.00
Your 5% 401(k) Plan Deduction	$ 2,000.00	$ 2,500.00
Employer 50% Matching	$ 1,000.00	$ 1,250.00
Total Paid Annually Employee 401(k) Participant Account	$ 3,000.00	$ 3,750.00

After 30 Years of Working with this Annual Contribution (and Assuming a Fixed Growth Rate) the Value Would Be:

With 6% Rate	$ 237,174.56	$ 296,468.20
With 8% Rate	$ 339,849.63	$ 377,584.60
With 10% Rate	$ 558,917.33	$ 682,287.84

◆ **403(b).** A non-profit organization, like a university, hospital, research foundation or charity, will typically offer this type of retirement option. It works similarly to a 401(k) plan, and also has a government-imposed maximum for 2005 contributions, which is $14,000.

◆ **Savings Incentive Match Plan for Employees (SIMPLE).** SIMPLE is another retirement plan typically offered by smaller companies. It too is similar to the 401(k), with a ceiling on how much can be invested annually. SIMPLE is not so simple. There are SIMPLE IRAs and SIMPLE 401(k)s. The limit for the SIMPLE IRA's in 2005 is $10,000, and $14,000 for the SIMPLE 401(k)s. These plans are easy for employers to set up but are very liberal regarding what employees must cover.

Hip Tip *We give a brief description of each below, but for more in-depth information, check out the "Show Me the Money" chapter of* THE HIP GIRL'S HANDBOOK FOR HOME, CAR & MONEY STUFF. *There you can also find out about* INDIVIDUAL RETIREMENT ACCOUNTS (IRAS) *in the event the company you work for doesn't offer a retirement plan.*

Employee Stock Option Plans (ESOP)

Oftentimes, a company will have a pension plan that serves as an additional means of pre-tax retirement savings for its employees (much like the more individualized 401(k), 403(b) and SIMPLE). In an ESOP plan, however, an employer allots a percentage of the company's profits to the ESOP fund, which gives you, the employee, shares of ownership in the company through company stock. As profits grow, so does your ownership in the company (and in some smaller businesses, employees might actually own the entire company). However, under an ESOP, you'll have to really show your loyalty to the company prior to reaping the rewards. Most companies' pension plans have a roll out of how much you can own based on your employment with the company. For instance, if you've worked for a company for three years, you may be 50 percent vested. This means that you own half of the stock you have secured from working at the company for three years. Therefore, if you left the company (or were forced out), you could walk away with only half of the money you'd invested, such as $30,000 of the $60,000 that your corporate stock's worth. (Keep in mind a company's stock can increase, stay steady or decline at any given moment.) When a company says you are "fully vested," that means you own 100 percent of the money you've accrued in your pension plan. It usually takes from five to ten years to become fully vested with a company.

Hip Tip *A stock is the purchase of a piece of the company. Stock prices can go up and down depending on the market, making you a profit or causing a loss of value in your stock investments. When you hear of a company that goes from privately owned to public — otherwise known as "going IPO" — this means that anyone, from the next-door-neighbor to your little sister, can now purchase stock in the company. In a privately owned for-profit corporation, only "internal" people, typically private investors and employees (who often take a lower salary hoping that the pay-off will be big when the company "goes public") can own stock in the company.*

Pension Plans

This is your company's retirement fund for you. There are two forms of pension plans:

◆ **Defined benefit pension plan.** This plan provides a target amount of the last five years of your salary to retire on. Let's say, in this case, 80 percent. This sort of plan requires the company to offer enough money to cover the employee's target account in the fund for your life span. As you can imagine, this is very costly for a company to establish and maintain.

◆ **Defined contributions pension plan.** In this plan, a company takes a percentage from its yearly profits (say 10 to 15 percent) and deposits the money into a fund for employees. The money is distributed at the end of each year, according to a ratio of your salary, against how many other employees must be covered, similar to how profit-sharing plans allocate contributions.

Stipend, Bonus or Employee Profit-sharing Plans

If the company's profits for the year are good, some companies may offer a pre-set formula that allows you to share in their extraordinary profits. A general formula might consist of a percentage of the company's profits based on your salary. Oftentimes, you have to belong to the management "club" to become eligible for this type of benefit. Keep in mind this is a good negotiating point if your salary isn't up to par. Negotiating a higher percentage, or being a recipient of such a perk, can bump your yearly earnings substantially.

Commission

This is the "extra" money, usually based on a percentage of the money an employee brings to the company as profit, that a company offers an employee as incentive to bring more money in to the company. Often, commissions are made at the time of a sale or profitable deal, or after meeting pre-specified quotas and sales. Oftentimes, a commission can raise an employee's annual salary by almost half of the base salary. Some jobs work solely on a commission basis, which means you do not get a base salary.

Sign-on Bonus

A company will sometimes give a hot-to-trot Hip Girl a chunk of change up front just to get her to agree to work for them. (Think of it like getting your allowance before you even do any work and then getting your regular allowance on top of that just to do your chores.) Usually, it comes with lots and lots of restrictions, time limits and a contract filled with ifs and buts; however, it can make taking a new job quite lucrative!

Overtime and Overtime Pay

Know whether you're an exempt or non-exempt employee to ensure your rights for overtime and overtime pay as mandated by federal and state laws under the Fair Labor Standards Act. This law requires companies to abide by certain salary and overtime specifications. Exemption status is how the Department of Labor classifies each job function so that it can determine if you, the employee who holds that position, are covered by the government-regulated work policies.

Generally speaking, most companies have very strict regulations regarding who is exempt and non-exempt, factoring in such variables as wages or duties. For example, two companies can call a person an administrative assistant, but the first company may be able to classify that person as exempt, while the second employer must classify that person as non-exempt. It's based on the duties of the job. Know your exemption status and what stipulations apply to your particular job. Your state's Department of Labor Website can help you sort it out.

Hip Tip *For some fields, like television news and media organizations, where freelancers (non-staff employees) are used frequently, your union may* require your employer to meet certain payment standards for various employer-requested services. Such union-enforced obligations might include time-and-a-half pay for each hour you work overtime, working holidays and a meal penalty (where you work through your lunch break). Such positions often require you to join a union. (For our purposes, we'll define union as a community of people who regulate corporate policies and compliance to these policies on behalf of individuals working in a specific field.) If that's you, be prepared to pay a hefty "joining" fee. And most important, inquire with your union's board to determine your rights.

Travel and Expense Reimbursement

Whether you travel by car, train, plane or automobile, ask your supervisor exactly what your company covers for travel and miscellaneous daily expenses that you might incur while working (like your astronomical cell phone bill or eating lunch in your cubicle while you work diligently on your report). Does the company have a corporate card you can use? This will keep you from having to dig deep into your pockets to shell out the cash for work-related expenses. If not, consider getting a separate credit card to use strictly for work-related expenses. This will help you keep better track of exactly what the company owes you.

Hip Tip *If you travel for work, ask if your company allows you to keep the frequent flier miles you earn for any air travel. Also, many credit cards partner with major hotel chains to offer points each time you stay at one of their hotels or use the partnering credit card that you can redeem for a free hotel stay. So if you're buying lunch or traveling on your company's dime, ask if you get to keep the bonus awards.*

Severance Packages

In most corporations, a severance package is set up to assist employees who lose their jobs due to unforeseen corporate challenges. This "benefit" is meant to help alleviate financial burdens while you look for other work. Most organizations have a pre-set formula for what an employee can get, usually dependent on years of service and your level of management. A sample severance package might be one week or one month paid for each year of service (up to a pre-set maximum), whereby someone who has worked for a company for four years might get one month of paid severance to look for another job. Typically, you do not get a severance package if you voluntarily resign from your position.

Hip Tip *If you're laid off or fired (unless, of course, it's due to willful misconduct like insubordination or theft) and you receive a severance package, negotiate to be paid for unused vacation and sick pay for which you're still eligible.*

Paid Leave/Time Off

The age-old saying, "All work and no play makes for a dull life," is definitely true. Sure, you might be passionate about your job as a pro-basketball player or a floral designer, but does it completely fulfill you? What about seeing the world, exercising, letting romance enliven you and building strong friendships? (Check out the "Great Balancing Act" chapter for more on that.) So despite the fact that you live and breathe the accomplishments from your work, taking time off is equally important to both your mental and physical health. And in the end, time off will make you a well-rounded, kindred spirit and generally lead to a much happier work demeanor (which your subordinates and colleagues will greatly appreciate).

◆ **Vacation days.** Exactly how many vacation days you get varies from company to company. It also often depends on how long you've worked with a company (with many companies working on an accrual system) and your  level, whether you're at the administration level or in management and above. Also, as usual, the company will often max out your paid vacation time no matter what your loyalty level. Most importantly, check with your HR rep or boss about whether your unused paid vacation days carry over to the next year or quarter. Vacation days are another negotiable factor prior to accepting a position or promotion.

Hip Tip *When requesting vacation days, make sure you've considered when is or is not a good time for you to take your vacation. For instance, if you work for a tax accountant and you know every April is your craziest time of the season, better schedule your trip to Florence after April 15. This increases your chances of getting a "yes" for your vacation request and shows your dedication toward your work.*

◆ **Sick days.** Nearly all companies, businesses and organizations offer paid sick days for full-time employees. We say, take these when necessary, because no one wants to catch a nasty cold or stomach flu from you. And sometimes, illnesses are not solely physical There are days when we're in need of serious "mental health" time off. Just use your sick days wisely. Even though a company may offer 10 sick days each year, a boss may cringe if you take nearly every single one of them. And remember, if you call in sick and it's due to a self-inflicted illness like a massive hangover, lay low. Don't flaunt your day off and accidentally run into a nosy co-worker at the gym.

◆ **Paid holidays.** Every calendar year has certain nationwide recognized holidays. Some organizations, like government jobs, honor most of them with the day off. It is at a public organization's discretion, however, to discern which (if any) holidays employees get off with pay. Widely recognized holidays include New Year's Day, Christmas, Memorial Day, Labor Day, Thanksgiving and the Fourth of July.

◆ **Personal or optional days.** Some businesses offer extra paid days off beyond holidays or vacations to take care of personal matters. How many varies with each organization. You do not have to tell your supervisor or HR representative why you're requesting personal days. However, granting your request is entirely up to them. And if you get 'em, girl, you better put 'em to use. Because like in fertility, if you don't use 'em, you lose 'em.

◆ **Bereavement leave.** Although not required, some companies extend employees paid time off in the event of the death of a close relative. How many days and how closely related you must be to qualify for this should be defined by your human resources team.

◆ **Marriage days.** So you're finally the bride and you can chuck your little black book filled with contact numbers of your Boytoys and Friends-with-Benefits. Oh, the memories! Not all corporations or organizations offer paid leave to celebrate your matrimonial bliss. But if you can get paid to get your groove on, girl, take full advantage of it!

Hip Tip   *If you're considering a new job or negotiating to stay with your current employer and you know you've got an important personal event for which you'll soon need time off, factor this into your negotiations. That way you'll be guaranteed the time off, whether paid or unpaid — and it might help you decide which job to take.*

◆ **Family and medical care paid coverage.** So you're the adoring new mommy of the world's most perfect child and you want and need some time to bond with your little rug rat. Whether you adopted, gave birth or were awarded legal guardianship of a child, you are eligible for time off according to the Family and Medical Leave Act (FMLA) federal law. The law requires an organization to offer a full-time employee up to 12 weeks of unpaid time off, and that secures your job for your return with full health benefits intact throughout this duration. This law also covers the need for temporary leave in order to take care of an immediate family member suffering from a critical illness or the like. Some companies offer paid time off for related matters.

◆ **Workers' Compensation.** Well, now that you know what Workers' Compensation Insurance is, know that it is within your rights to get paid time off from your job if you are injured while working, as long as you fall (pardon the pun) within the state law requirements for such benefits. This will require, however, a letter saying so from your doctor. Additionally, should you feel that your manager is retaliating against you for filing a claim — like with a hostile attitude, termination or unnecessary disciplinary recourse — it's within your rights to bring about legal action for this unjust behavior.

Pitch for the Perks

We've just covered the basics a company or organization might offer you. But in today's highly skilled pool of candidates, many corporations are going above and beyond to recruit and keep qualified people happy. Below are some perks you might encounter, and if not, some that you might want to consider negotiating. But before you do, let us remind you to do your homework. Check what is prevalent in your industry, because you'd hate to look like a fool and request a perk that in no way fits your industry's work environment.

◆ **Jury duty, witness service or election day pay.** Many companies supplement or cover days off when you support your governmental responsibilities, up to a pre-set maximum. And if you are paid by the government, oftentimes your office may ask you to sign your government-issued check over to them to help alleviate the company's cost for covering your entire pay.

◆ **Earth Day/Volunteer Day.** In an effort to encourage employees to take care of their environment and community, many corporations support a day or two off each year with pay for employees to devote themselves to a clean-up or other volunteer effort.

◆ **Educational assistance and reimbursement.** From pursuing a higher degree, like your master's in business, to taking credible extension or certification courses related to your job function, many companies may cover a portion to all of your costs related to the pursuit of higher education. Inquire with your boss and the HR department for the details of your company's plan.

Hip Tip *There are other smart ways for you to save up to pay for your or your family's higher education expenses in the event your company doesn't have a program that pays it for you. The 529 College Savings Plan is an employee-deposited college fund devised by the government whereby the employee enables the company to automatically withdraw a specified amount of pre-taxable income from each paycheck and put it into the 529 fund. The investment grows while in the fund, and withdrawals to cover qualified college expenses are free from federal income tax, but not always state income tax. The fund can be opened by you or any relative, such as a parent, grandparent, aunt, sibling or even a close friend. The owner controls the distribution and deposits in the fund (which maxes out at much higher limits than most other educational funds). Another employee-contributed educational fund is the Coverdell Education Savings Account (ESA). ESAs, too, are tax-deferred income options to pay for educational expenses, but due to the particulars of ESAs — where you can buy and sell whatever you want whenever you want — it might be best to allocate an ESA fund for private school education and the 529 plan specifically for college. Consult your financial advisor for what might be best for you.*

◆ **Flex-time.** Perhaps your company offers a half-day Friday with a full-day's pay, a split work week with another professional (known as job-share), a convenient work-from-home schedule, a work exchange program with your company's Australian office or the technologically advanced telecommuting option. If your company doesn't offer them, why not write a proposal to negotiate them for yourself? If you don't ask, you'll never know what might have been.

◆ **Corporate sabbaticals.** Some companies, educational institutions, dot.com and Fortune 500 professions are incorporating sabbatical leave into their benefits in an attempt to attract and retain strong talent. During sabbatical leave, salary and benefits usually continue while the employee agrees to work with the organization for a pre-specified period of time.

◆ **Employee Assistance Programs (EAPs).** Many larger companies offer various forms of confidential programs to help employees deal with individual, family, community and workplace crises and other unforeseen catastrophes. Some companies act simply as a referral program, whereas other companies have full crisis programs they pay for in case employees need them. Some different forms of EAP programs include childbirth and rearing, like prenatal, adoption and childcare services; emergency, special needs and summer care programs; mental and physical healthcare counseling programs; and educational/well-being seminars. Ask your company about all that is offered. It'll help you get the biggest bang for your work efforts.

◆ **Employee discounts.** Many companies offer employee discounts toward their products. It's smart business, really, as it is a shameless promotion of their goods. So if you work at Levi's and get a serious 30 percent discount on your jeans, or J. Crew and benefit from the "Friends and Family" discount day, use it to help you complete your work-savvy wardrobe for cheap!

◆ **Moving or relocating pay.** If you're moving halfway across the country to take up your new role as manager of the southern region of Target, make sure to propose and secure that the company pay for the move. Request that they pay for all expenses related to your move, including gas mileage, movers, and a plane ticket and hotel for you to scout the area to determine where to set up residence. Make sure to figure all expenses you might incur if you were to accept the promotion before agreeing to an overall relocation-reimbursement budget. If you've just bought a condo or home across town, and your company won't pay for your move, they may offer one or two paid days off to help you get your life together. Check it out or request it so you don't have to use one of your personal or optional days to haul your heavy load.

◆ **Gym memberships.** In an effort to promote a healthy lifestyle for its employees (and to make working out more convenient so you can stay in the office longer without feeling guilty), many companies have gym facilities in their buildings, or even offer personal instructors. Those that don't offer at-work health programs often offer discounts on memberships with nearby gyms.

◆ **Plethora of pickin's.** A company can offer as many or as few perks as it wants, and we've seen some companies go all out for employees with laundry service, catered meals and so on. Take full advantage of the freebies your company offers, and don't be afraid to push the envelope every so often to encourage them to re-visit their current benefits package. What a great way to be a modern-day Erin Brockovich!

———◈———

What a business offers in benefits and perks is often equally important as what it pays for your hard work. Investigate all your options! You never know what you're paying for out of your own pocket that your company could be paying for instead.

Nailing the Negotiations:
Getting the Salary, Promotion, Relocation or Job Switch You Desire

"My boyfriend and I were in the middle of planning a month-long vacation to New Zealand when I landed an interview with an amazing company. I was torn between canceling the trip to start immediately or asking if I could do both. I didn't want to lose out on this great opportunity, but I also knew I wouldn't get a month off to travel once I started working. On my second interview, I decided to try to negotiate the trip into my contract. And what do you know? It actually worked!"

Eliana, 23, Travel and Event Associate

Generally speaking, long gone are the days companies take care of employees the way they took care of our parents and grandparents. Today's competitive job market will likely require you to fight for that pay increase, title promotion, relocation or switch from sales to marketing. But since we can't all afford lawyers or agents to negotiate for us what we want from our careers (besides, the battle scars are what make us warriors in the boardroom), we Hip Girls will have to step up to bat for ourselves.

More Bang for Your Buck: Getting the Salary You Deserve

Whether you're fresh out of high school or college and looking to get the most money for your educational knowledge, or you've been with your company for several years and your income isn't what you'd hoped for by now, learning how to successfully persuade your employer to pay you the money you feel you deserve can be nerve-racking. After all, no one really likes to part with money.

◆ **Do your homework** and document your value to the company and the overall industry. Find out how much you're worth in the market. This is determined by several factors, including your field, your educational background, your previous work experience, the region where you're working, and the economic climate in your industry and at your company.

Hip Tip WORKING WOMAN *magazine publishes an annual salary survey that covers dozens of fields. Log onto www.workingwoman.com for more information. Other publications and trade-specific newsletters and magazines also publish salary ranges and surveys. A few online sources include www.jobstar.org, www.wageweb.com and www.salary.com. But to proactively combat employers' side-stepping tactics, contact the HR department of your company's competitive businesses and inquire what the salary range is for your title (or the one you're vying for).*

◆ **Highlight and factor in your "softer skills"** or "proven successes." It'll make you stronger against stiff competition. (Think of it like when you were teenager and you waged a "take no prisoners" war about why you instead of your older brother deserved the family car for the night.) Offer examples. Maybe you're fresh off graduation, but you've been working in a related customer-service industry part-time. Or, if you're currently employed, point out how you've established solid relationships with your company's executives, vendors and clients and have surpassed your sales quotas for the last four quarters.

◆ **Next, prepare viable options you'd consider** when met with resistance. Whether you're simply a candidate for the position or an employee with a proven track record, head into the negotiations knowing what your bottom figure is and what other "perks" you'd consider in order to accept that figure.

HipTip *Some of the perks might include extra paid vacation time, work-from-home Fridays, relocation fees, a bonus or commission, or a piece of the company once it goes "public." (Look at the "Human Resources Breakdown" chapter for more ideas.)*

◆ **Let the negotiations begin.** If you're applying for a new job, wait for your potential employer to offer a salary figure. If you're asked what you want, throw the lead back in their lap by saying, "What is the salary range of the position?" If they still insist that you offer up your salary request first, give them a reasonable range — based on your experience and your competitive salary research. Make your range a flexible one, dependent on what your benefits package includes. For example: "I think a fair salary range for this job, due to my experience, is between $62K and $67K, contingent on the specifics of the benefits package." Make sure the low end of your range is just slightly above what you really want and need to make (in this case we'll say $60K) and is on par with the fair market value of the position. This will keep you from pricing yourself out of the job, but still give you room to negotiate without getting stuck with your bottom dollar. Be cautious to not make your range overly broad.

Hip Tip   *Avoid disclosing your current salary whenever you apply for a new gig. If you're asked what your current salary is, reply, "I would expect my salary to reflect the market rate for this position and my (list your key softer skills here) experience. According to my research, that is between $75K and $80K." If a potential employer investigates with your former employer what your last salary was, larger companies will give a pay range for that specific role, like, "That level of employee makes between $70K and $80K." But not all companies have strict policies on an appropriate response and may divulge facts you'd rather leave unspoken. However, if pressed, honesty is the best policy. Just make sure to add that you feel "the particular skills or experience" you bring to the position make you worth XX more money.*

If you're currently employed and negotiating for a pay increase, strategically request a meeting with your boss. Pick a date that might increase your chances for a yes. A rule of thumb may be to make a date with your supervisor at least one month before your annual review. Sometimes your boss may need to work out a raise with HR or find room in the budget.

☐ Ask to meet on a Thursday or Friday, if possible. This will give everyone some space apart — especially important if the negotiations don't go well.

☐ Ask to meet toward the end of the day or after work. Do not make it a lunch meeting.

☐ In general lines of business, don't ask for a raise if it's been less than six months since your last pay increase or performance review.

☐ If you work in freelance or own your own business, keep your hikes or rates comparable to your last or similar job.

HipTip *Strategy is the name of the game when it comes to asking for a raise. Why wait until your annual review? Consider asking for more money shortly after you nail a really big client or do phenomenally well on a project. They'll likely be more receptive to the idea. Another good time is mid-year, where you have the opportunity to increase your salary once before your annual review — thereby possibly sneaking in two raises in a year.*

◆ **Sell them on a pay increase** using your great presentation skills. Regardless of whether you're interviewing for the job or you're already a star employee, it's important to broach your salary request in a style that uses poise, proof and shows confidence in yourself. If your delivery rings of any uncertainty, you can bet they'll question it too. And just like a dog that's attacked will fight back, if you broach your request in a demanding, criticizing manner, there's a good chance your manager will feel attacked and respond similarly.

HipTip *Manipulating or intimidating your boss into giving you a pay increase will only make him or her angry and resistant. Always be*

professional in your delivery. Exhibiting any of the following behaviors will dimin-
ish your credibility and chances of getting the salary you want:

Avoiding	Snubbing
Belittling	Suffering in silence
Blustering	Teasing
Nagging	Threatening
Ridiculing	Using sarcasm
Scolding	Whining

◆ **Carefully listen to your boss's reply.** Respond accordingly. If the person in charge of your income is clearly not agreeing to your terms, ask that person to clarify why. But if you easily receive a yes, honey, get it in writing and give yourself a hand.

◆ **Let's assume they say no citing a generic reason** like the company doesn't have a raise in the budget. Here is where you put your negotiation skills to the test. You can say, "The money is important to me, but I like working here (or I want to work here). Therefore, I'd like to discuss additional compensation options that might meet your budget constraints and mine." You can then consider lowering your dollar figure enough to show you're making an effort to compromise by saying, "I understand your position. I can make $50K work for my base if I can get an extra seven days of paid vacation each year to compensate for the difference in pay."

◆ **If you and your supervisor or HR representative have come to an agreement,** be sure to ask when you can expect your pay increase or other alternatives to "kick in." If your boss agrees to push for a pay increase for you, but can't make any promises, be sure to let her know your timeframe for letting you know. In the meantime, don't be shy (but don't be pushy either) about checking in with her occasionally — once every six weeks or so, depending on your timeframe.

What to Do if Your Salary Negotiations are a One-way Street

All right, you feel like you're banging your head against a brick wall (girl, we've all been there before, trust us). What can you do if your manager (or potential employer) is being stubborn, and you seem to be driving the negotiations with no help from him—or her? Try these tactics:

◆ **Request a performance review** six months prior to your next review. Here, you must tell your boss how much you want to earn and ask what you need to do to get there, drafting the specific goals and expectations he will use as markers for getting the increase in pay you desire.

◆ **Seek out a position at the competition.** As in love, your boss may not fully appreciate what he has in you until he risks losing you to someone else. Actively search for another position at a company, particularly one that directly competes with your current employer. Then privately tell your supervisor that you're entertaining an offer from them. Make sure to reinforce that you haven't yet made up your mind because you really like working for her and the company. Wait for her to ask if you'd consider a counter offer. If she doesn't, you may be forced to suggest it, saying something like: "I'd like to stay. Are you open to discussing an increase in my base salary (or a promotion)?"

Hip Tip *Don't threaten to quit or walk out. It'll only come back to haunt you. Your employer could respond with a, "Feel free to show yourself out the door." If you're going to play the high-power game, you gotta come prepared to walk away. So make sure the other deal you're entertaining is a job you feel good about taking.*

◆ **Like in buying a car, you might have to "walk away"** if the deal-making isn't going your way. We know it's scary, but completely giving in on all your needs and desires rarely makes any job worth taking. Weigh your personal needs — like if you just need the money to get you by until you find the job that will pay what you're worth — against walking away. If it's meant to be, it will.

Hip Tip *Never actually say what your personal needs are that require you to have the salary you're requesting. A past-due mortgage payment, diapers or saving up to help your little brother go to college in no way affects the company's bottom line. Keep your negotiations about business at all times.*

◆ **Get your agreed-upon negotiation in writing.** Otherwise, the passing of time may bring the passing of memory. It makes it too easy for the boss to relegate her forgetfulness to a "miscommunication," then you can kiss your extra week's vacation (and all your hard negotiations) goodbye.

Passing the Baton — Negotiating the Promotion and Relocation You Want

Long before the negotiations for a promotion or new office begin, you'll have to plead your case as to why you're worthy of it (just like any guy who wants to date or marry you has to prove he deserves you). Provide both tangible (increase in clients, nailed big stories, highest sales or taking on additional responsibilities) and intangible (the softer skills we cover in *Smart & Savvy Strategies for Success, Working Your Assets, Colleague Camaraderie* and *Boss Behavior*).

Combine both your tangible and intangible successes to make a power presentation. Here is how to maneuver the negotiations.

◆ **What have you done for them lately?** Base your answer not on what you want, but on what your employer deems as stellar work performance. Just as you shouldn't request a larger salary simply because you want to sport a new SUV, wanting a fancy new title and a better parking space aren't reasons for your boss to promote you. You must first consistently demonstrate success and professional behavior. You say you're not a mind reader; how do you know what they consider promotion-worthy behavior? Look around your immediate department. Have other colleagues been promoted? When and why? Did they earn master's degrees or have they beat their sales quota repeatedly during the past year? Do they have a great relationship with the boss? How's yours? What's your success rate? If you still can't clearly determine if you've delivered results and exhibited the behavior that your company considers favorable, ask your supervisor what qualities she looks for in someone at the next level. Then compare your skill level and office manners with her expectations to help you discern if you've got a shot at a promotion.

Hip Tip   *For additional qualities employers look for when considering whether or not to promote a subordinate, check out* The Career Survival Guide *by Brian O'Connell. This author offers a great list of "do's and don'ts" for working your way up the leadership ladder.*

◆ **Gather proof.** From formal memos, to an analysis of your competition's status, to sales sheets or emails of praise, offer strong examples — anything that documents your achievements — to support your cause. Just make sure materials are relatively recent and from respected professional sources.

Do convince your manager to create a position for you. Whether your department is already top-heavy or you're following your husband who accepted a job in Washington, D.C., if it makes sense in your business, see if they're willing to work with you to keep you. If you'd like to stay with your company and your company considers you invaluable, propose a new role or title, such as sending you to open their East Coast branch. Put your proposal in writing. The computer program Bizplan offers an automatic format for you to follow to write your own business proposal and can easily be installed in your computer. Patrick Riley's book THE ONE-PAGE PROPOSAL: HOW TO GET YOUR BUSINESS PITCH ONTO ONE PERSUASIVE PAGE *also offers great tips.*

◆ **Walk in your boss's moccasins.** Think how or why he might meet your request with resistance and prepare a reasonable rebuttal for each possible objection. Whenever possible, support your position with proof.

Timing is key to life. Consider what unforeseen obstacles your boss might have to confront if he were to promote you or help you relocate. Some challenges your boss might have to consider are: Will the company appear to be playing favorites with one department, individual or coast if they promote you? Is the company losing money and laying off employees? Would your new role come with additional expenses like an assistant or new overhead charges such as rent? These are important factors for determining if your request will be answered now, later or never.

◆ **Next, review the Salary Negotiations** portion of this chapter. From this point forward, it serves as your guideline for requesting a promotion. As a refresher:

    ☐ Strategically request a meeting with your boss.

- Sell him or her on the idea with your great presentational skills.
- Listen to your boss's response.

◆ **Prepare to negotiate.** Follow the format outlined above under What to Do if Your Salary Negotiations are a One-way Street, and tailor your rebuttal according to your promotion or relocation needs. As a quick review, these steps include:

- Request a review. In the case of a promotion or relocation request, plant your seed early enough in the game to allow your boss to make it happen. Revisiting her status is equally important, so check back with her every three to four months about her progress.

Hip Tip *Offer a proposed timeframe for meeting your request. If you leave your proposal with an open-ended deadline, chances are your boss may take her time arranging her schedule to accommodate your request. While you shouldn't press her based solely on your timeline, it is important to propose a range of time that you think is reasonable and fair. Say, "I'd like to be promoted in the next quarter," or "I'm moving with my family to Denver in June. If possible, I'd love to know whether opening the regional office there is an option by the end of March so that if it doesn't pan out, I can look for work elsewhere." Be polite, but clear with your request.*

- Seek out a position at the competition. Especially in the case of a promotion, you may need to secure a job with your company's rival in order to remind your company the value of your time, skill and work ethic. In the case of a relocation, you can't fly on promises alone. Until you've worked out the details of your relocation, keeping your options open in the area is equally important to landing on your feet. Put your feelers out for work before you have to.

Hip Tip *Don't rub your boss's nose in your straying eye. You don't want to see your husband flirt with the waitress. Don't "tease" your boss either. If you're asking for a promotion, go about seeking a position with your competition quietly, until you've secured an offer from them. If you've begun your job hunt because of your pending relocation proposal, politely inform your boss that you're "reaching out" in case the proposal doesn't work out. But make sure to reassure her that you'll keep her in the loop if a substantial offer pops up before the relocation details have been solidified.*

☐ Prepare to walk away. If your timeframe isn't meeting your boss's, or if she's being flaky about her decision, know your limit. If you stay too long in a position that you feel is taking advantage of you, you'll only grow to resent your company and your boss. Don't take that chance. Get out while the feelings are still amicable.

☐ Get your negotiations in writing. Like in a marriage proposal, the deal ain't signed, sealed and delivered until the ceremony's over.

Getting the Itch to Job-Switch

So teaching fifth grade has lost its luster and you want to refresh your career by taking on the little kindergarten monsters. Or you're spent as a cashier and want to work in the pharmacy division. Switching roles within your company is a great way to keep the job passion alive without too much risk.

◆ **Start by looking around** at the other divisions or departments. Are there any that pique your interest? If not, skip to the *Big "O" — Opportunity* chapter. You're going to have to look outside your company to find your new passion.

◆ **Gently drop the news to your boss** that you're curious about what the promotion and special events department does. We know, this can be kind of scary, especially if you have a boss who isn't very supportive of your career growth. But it's important to let her know you've been investigating your options outside the department rather than have her hear it from a colleague. If we haven't stressed it enough, how you position your interest with her is of critical importance. Do it in a way that reinforces your commitment and loyalty to your job. Try, "I've worked here for a couple years and I'm not clear what the promotions department does. Considering that we work closely with them, I was thinking it would be good if I understood their role better. Do you mind if I ask Mr. Robbins' assistant if I can sneak in for a quick meet-n-greet?" Hopefully, the boss will be supportive.

◆ **Request a meet-n-greet with a management-level person** in the field you're interested in learning more about. Work within their schedule. Remember, they're doing you a favor.

◆ **If your boss puts the kibosh on your request** for an informational interview and she doesn't offer to make the call for you, get a clue. This lady probably isn't going to help you get anywhere soon. You can suck it up and look outside the company discreetly. You can also ask your mentor for help. Or you can take it to your HR department. Just remember, not all things are confidential with them.

◆ **With your boss's blessing,** prepare for the one-on-one informational meeting. As in a job interview, have a list of generic questions prepared. This will help him give you the answers you're looking for.

◆ **Be professional at all times** during your informational interview, including in your speech, dress and attitude. Don't reveal ugly things about your boss or department if you're not happy. Remember, you are there to listen. Soak it up.

◆ **At the end of the meeting thank him for his time.** If you liked what you discovered, here's where you can build a new contact. Ask if you can contact him in the future if you have additional questions or ideas.

◆ **Follow up with a thank you.** Either a handwritten note or an email will suffice.

◆ **Report back to your boss** that you learned a great deal and feel confident it will benefit your current position. But if you think you want to slide departments, mention it, very delicately, to your supervisor. Position it like, "I'm really intrigued by what Mr. Robbins had to say and I think one day I might like to work in that department." This will gently put your boss on the alert that you've got your feelers out without jumping ship and leaving her high and dry. That, after all, is a sure way to burn a bridge in both your current job and with your new contact.

◆ **Nurture your new contact.** Make a point to say "hi" to him in meetings, befriend his assistant, forward him your résumé and throw in an occasional stop-by once a month or so when you "happen to be walking by his office." Just don't become a nuisance. It's a fine line between persistence and stalking. (You've dated long enough to know exactly what we're talking about!)

◆ **Meanwhile, if you learned during your informational meeting** that you would require additional education, special certification or skills, do all you can to obtain such skills and experience during your "day job." After all, this is a sign of dedication toward a chance to get ahead. And anytime you get a step closer to the job function you're jockeying for, make sure to mention it to your new contact.

⚊⚊⚎⚏⚎⚊⚊

We know negotiating isn't easy. But if, as in life, you don't take a risk and ask for what you want, you'll never know just what you may have lost.

Career Couture:

Fashion Tips For Dressing For Success

—◦◦◦—

"I woke up late for work and threw on a cute skirt, heels and scarf to match the Paul Frank baby-tee I'd just slept in the night before. My hair was sporting a total bed-head style. I topped off my fashionably disheveled look by applying a little powder, mascara and lipstick as I frantically drove to work. Upon my arrival, and much to my chagrin, my boss scurried me into a big meeting with him and a potential client . . . even looking like I did! When the meeting came to a close, the client complimented me on my morning's fashion statement, and my boss followed suit by gushing about my impeccable sense of style. Go figure!"

—Mary, 27, Beauty Marketing Director

You love the fashion found in the pages of *Lucky* and *Vogue* magazines. But trust us, if you show up in your pharmacy break room sporting Christian Dior knock-off sunglasses or appear at your company's afternoon barbecue in your barely-there mini-skirt with stilettos, you'll quickly become the laughingstock of your colleagues. Your personal style — from your hair to your clothing and make-up — communicate a lot about you to other people. It may not seem fair that you're judged on your appearance, and that your work performance alone doesn't speak of your competence. But we are an image nation, and your bosses, clients and colleagues will project certain values, work ethics and personality traits onto you based solely on your appearance. And while we advocate that a Hip Girl dress in a manner that is true to her identity, we also recognize that sometimes you have to tone your assets down (or play them up) to assist you in achieving your career aspirations.

Fashion Gambling: Stacking the Cards in Your Favor

Whether you're in a casual work environment where you can wear sneakers, a manicurist in charge of her dress code or an attorney whose clothing has to scream of authority, a Hip Girl dresses strategically for her role by abiding by the unofficial office fashion code. But a Hip Girl also knows that wearing or doing what everybody else does won't make her stand out in a crowd as a leader; so she infuses her work-safe wardrobe with a distinctly individual style. Use the key factors below to help you survey your own workplace fashion landscape and to build your own appropriate, but personalized, work-wardrobe.

◆ **First, be clear on who's checking you out** (no, we don't just mean the hottie at the coffee shop). Are you meeting a new client and encouraging her to invest her money with your brokerage firm? Are you a new boss with employees who look to you to set the standard or are judging you before you've even given your first mandate? Maybe you're a role model for an intern or a little girl who's never had anyone to mentor her career fashion. Figure out who your audience is, and dress according to their needs as much as your own.

Hip Tip *Some days your role will change, depending on what's going on in your work world. For instance, a teacher will dress differently on Parents' Night than on a regular school day, or a businesswoman might get spiffed up more than usual if she knows she has to present at a meeting. We suggest you keep a Palm Pilot or a day planner to monitor what's happening in your work schedule so you can dress to impress your ever-changing clientele.*

◆ **Next, identify the standard attire in your office.** What are the other women wearing? Especially take note of the women who are the movers and shakers. After all, if you ever hope to fill their stilettos, consider emulating their fashion sense and work styles and then infusing these with your own individual strengths.

Hip Tip *Casual dress days are all about comfort. But before stepping one foot outside your door, ask yourself if you'd be comfortable meeting the CEO of your company in your outfit. A Hip Girl must be ready for any situation at anytime.*

◆ **Invest your money in the pieces that seem consistent with your job.** A basic black suit, khakis, a company-issued uniform or a pair of gray pin-striped slacks might get the most wear (or if you've landed your dream magazine gig, perhaps the standard is the latest pair of designer jeans. Sweet!). The key is to own several quality pieces of the office standard that differ in style, cut, fit or color. For instance, if dress slacks are your standard item, invest in choices that are slightly different in flair, cut, fit or color.

◆ **Buy clothes that fit you now.** We know that may seem like a no-brainer. But let's be real. How many of us have purchased a pair of pants or a skirt a size too small in the hopes our low-fat, low-carb, turbo-charged diet will have a big payoff? Maybe it will, but don't try to squeeze yourself into clothes that don't fit and try to look good. 'Cuz girl, let us tell you what your friends aren't going to: Live in the moment and make do with what you have. If you weren't born with Cameron Diaz's lanky body or with Beyoncé's bootilicious features, chances are no amount of sweat and exercise or plastic surgery is going to give you something you were never meant to have. Buy appropriately sized clothes that accentuate your assets (see more on that below), but that are loose enough in case you pack on a few pounds during a hell week at work.

◆ **Stretch your wardrobe dollar** by making your wardrobe versatile. Variety is the spice of life. In a smart-casual environment, don't dump all your money into two super expensive suits and elegant, but pricey tops. Maximize your moolah. Extend your wardrobe options by buying a quality suit with a variety of nice tops, a skirt and a sport jacket. Then pair them up differently to make it look like you have all-new outfits. And don't forget to buy accessories. Accessories can disguise your usual outfit as a whole new purchase.

Hip Tip   *Author Brian O'Connell says in his book* THE CAREER SURVIVAL GUIDE *that up to 95 percent of the time employees are judged for hiring or promotion during the first few minutes of visual contact. If you're a virgin to the professional work world, up for a promotion or making your debut as a guest speaker, play it safe by dressing smart casual. Some key articles include a nice pair of dress slacks or a near knee-length tailored skirt with a nicely fitted top that doesn't expose an overflowing cleavage. Heels and a well-tailored blazer always dress up a casual top and slacks.*

◆ **Dress professionally comfortable.** You're there to work and win your clients over. If you're a teacher, you'll have a hard time playing kickball in a pair of heels. The more comfortable you feel, the more focused you'll be on the task at hand. Keep your look professional, but comfortable. If you're going to be on your feet all day, wear a low heel or flats. Be sensibly comfortable. A J-Lo or Juicy Couture jumpsuit might fly in the newsroom, but if an opportunity to cover a breaking story arises, chances that the assignment editor will send you out in public to represent the station are low. (And you've lost your first chance to prove yourself because of what you're wearing!) All we're saying is looking good while feeling good is essential.

◆ **Finally, choose age-appropriate pairings.** Unless you're Madonna (whose job it is to shock people), wearing clothes that compliment your age will garner respect from your co-workers. A good rule of thumb is to fluctuate within a three to five year mark — whether older or younger depends on your age bracket and industry. Baring a little skin or accessorizing with fringe might fly at work, but your older colleagues may label you as immature based solely on your appearance. Unfortunately, this will likely affect the type of responsibilities you're given. Age yourself up five years if you're in your early 20s (unless of course you're an actress and you're on an audition to play a high-schooler on Broadway). But if you're 35 and you've earned a lot more respect and have more responsibility in the workforce, leave the leather choker at home and opt for a scarf to sexify your button-down top. As you mature, so should your wardrobe. That doesn't mean you have to look stodgy or can't appear sexy. Age appropriate dressing is about being selective when you choose to display your sex appeal — like opting for a form-fitting twin-set sweater instead of a risqué tank and jean jacket.

Hip Tip *Go ahead. Be a little girl again. Grab a trusted girlfriend or two and play dress-up one weekend. Tear apart your closet to test your fashion boundaries. You'll learn what works and what items you need to purchase to pull your wardrobe together. When you and your fashion-savvy girlfriends figure out what works, snap photos of your outfits and varied looks. Then scrapbook them according to the style (business casual, meetings, event day, etc.) so you don't have to sweat what works and what doesn't during your hectic work week.*

How to Be a Fashion Maverick

Once you've determined your work-safe wardrobe staples, dare to stand out as a fashion maverick. Below are some tips on how to safely incorporate your personality into your office closet:

◆ **Infuse your personal flair** with accessories. Belts, purses, earrings, pins, necklaces, scarves, ties, bracelets and shoes are where you can showcase your true self in the office. Remember, less is more when it comes to accessorizing. Not all of us look as good as Beyoncé with all that Bling-Bling.

Hip Tip *If you're in a conservative environment or don't know the fashion climate, keep your outfit tuned into more neutral, work-safe colors — like black, brown, tan, white or gray — until you become certain of the dress code. Then let your accessories announce your personal flavor by adding a pop of color with your handbags, shoes, belt, ladybug print scarf or bold necklace.*

◆ **Blend the trendy smartly.** Whether you're updating your classic look with a trendy accessory, like a pair of hoop earrings or bangle bracelet, or through a staple, like a button-down top featuring an in-the-now ruffle or leather trim — here's where you make or break your fashion statement. Incorporate only one or two trendy pieces per outfit. Unless you're auditioning to be a Pamela Anderson impersonator, pairing leather pants and a trendy bustier together for the office doesn't exactly say, "Trust my judgment."

Hip Tip   *Don't spend a ton of money on trendy items. Discount and chain stores like Target, Marshall's, Forever 21 and Ross offer huge savings on designer and cool-looking fashion items. And if you really find yourself in a pinch for clothing cash, check out www.ebay.com to bid for that perfect black dress for your work-related cocktail party. Your local Salvation Army (www.salvationarmy.org), Goodwill (www.goodwill.org) or second-hand boutiques often offer killer pieces that make old outfits look brand new. You can also flip to the yellow pages under Clothing, Retail Shops, and Used or Second-hand. Or perhaps there's a non-profit organization in your area that helps lower-income women with professional work attire and skills, like DRESS FOR SUCCESS, which has over 75 affiliates across the country and in some foreign countries as well. Log onto www.DressforSuccess.org to see if there's an affiliate near you, or look under Women's Organizations or Women's Non-profits in your yellow pages.*

◆ **Mix-n-match wisely.** It's fun to throw a little twist into your everyday work outfit. So if you're in the mood to show off your sassy side — and your creative work space applauds you for your brazen fashion style — consider pairing unlikely patterns, colors and fabrics together that scream, "Wow, that Hip Girl knows how to pull herself together."

◆ **Kick up your heel-power.** Comfort is important no matter what your profession, whether you're a nurse, businesswoman or physical therapist. But a Hip Girl invests in the pair of tennis shoes, heels or loafers that offers both  great support and style. Shoes complete the outfit, after all. So buy shoes that are unique in style, color or pattern. And if you've got a jaunt to work or you've got some down time between meetings, take a lesson from New York and San Francisco residents. Swap out your fancy dress shoes with tennies until it's time to make your debut on set or at the meeting. And remember, shoe care is equally important as shoe style.

◆ **The big briefcase theory.** Whether you're lugging a purse, briefcase, laptop backpack or Hip Girl handbag for your everyday work baggage, make it more than an investment; make it a fashion accessory. Invest in a sturdy and closure-smart workbag, but girl, use it to work your Hip Girl fashion magic. Consider investing in at least two workbags: one that's cross-color trendy (denim and leather tend to be multi-color friendly) and another that's travel-smart, yet fashionable.

◆ **Fine-tune your engine.** No ladies, we're not talking about your vehicle but your clothes. Take a close look. Is your shirt spot-free, ironed and tucked in? Does it reek of smoke from last night's social gathering? Are your shoes shined or all scuffed up? Are your nylons snagged or sagging something fierce? Can you see your thong underwear when you bend over? Do you have any deodorant smeared on your shirt? Are your nails noticeably chipped or uneven? It's the details, after all, that set a Hip Girl apart from the rest. You don't just look (and smell) good; you clearly take pride in presenting your best appearance!

Hip Tip *Don't underestimate the power of a good manicure. A Hip Girl who feels pulled together is more likely to extend a firm, confident hand-shake. We gals know that badly chipped or uneven nails can actually affect how we feel about ourselves. Presenting a polished, au natural appearance looks much better than trying to pass off those nastily chipped nails.*

The Psychology of a Good Bra

There's an old saying: You are what you eat. The same can be said about what you wear. What you look like on the outside is a reflection of how you feel on the inside. Think about it. Why else do we gals rush out to buy cute, new workout clothes to jumpstart our exercise routines? Or better yet, why do we need a matching lacy, racy fire engine red bra and panty set when our good ol' granny underwear is much more comfortable? Because we want to feel a certain way about ourselves: sexy, smart, strong and beautiful. If you feel good about your looks, you will project a happier, healthier, stronger, more confident attitude. Even if you're no Cindy Crawford or Kate Moss (and let's face it, most of us aren't anywhere near super-model material), it's what you do with what God gave you — physically, emotionally, spiritually and intellectually — that makes you feel and look attractive.

◆ **Know your physical assets.** A Hip Girl uses her strengths, like street-smarts, intellect, charm and personality, to help win over her clients. (See the "Working Your Assets" chapter for more details.) Knowing your most powerful physical attributes is key. For example, people may become mesmerized by your beautiful eyes or voluminous hair. Perhaps you've got a beaming smile that turns heads, or your long, lean legs are the envy of women everywhere. Figure out what you love most about your appearance and listen closely to what others genuinely compliment you on. Sometimes we are blind to our own attributes. Feedback from both friends and strangers can help us to own (and hone) our strongest features. So if friends appropriately compliment you on your curvaceous body, don't brush it off like they're crazy! Make a mental note of it. They may be pointing out an asset you never knew you had.

◆ **Play up two or three of your most precious physical assets.** Your appearance is also your résumé, after all. Highlight your most attractive features to magnify your office presence. So go ahead, wear a push-up bra underneath that turtleneck sweater or go for the sleeveless mock that shows off your rock-solid Madonna arms. Flexing your outer beauty is not a sin. When done tactfully, it's a smart strategy.

HipTip *If in doubt about what looks good on you, consider getting a personal shopper to help you. Some department stores offer personal shoppers who hand select outfits for you based on your size, personal style, event need and lifestyle. It works like this: Personal shoppers typically are of no expense to you. They work off commissions that the store pays them in return for any sales they make. You make an appointment and give them all the details of your needs. If you go in for a meeting and decide nothing works for you, you can walk out empty-handed without owing a dime. Once you've clicked with your personal shopper, he'll call* periodically with sale info or new inventory that's perfect for your wardrobe. Check out Marshall Field's (www.marshallfields.com), Nordstrom's (1-888-282-6060 or www.nordstroms.com), Henri Bendel's in New York (212/247-1100) or Saks (1-877-551-SAKS or www.saks.com) to find a store near you, and request to speak with a personal shopper or someone in their client services department.

◆ **Don't turn your assets into flaws.** Overdoing the "look at me" quotient at work will quickly turn your appearance into an office disturbance. You don't want your overexposed assets to give people at your work the chance to stereotype you before you've had a chance to prove your talent and skills. So play up your assets carefully. This Hip Girl author once had to ask an assistant to cover up her new pride-and-joys. The assistant's physical assets were in danger of becoming flaws. Women in the office were put off by her overflowing cleavage while the men assumed she was ditsy before she even opened her mouth. After our little discussion, she was careful to wear shirts that covered her cleavage but that were still form-fitting and accentuated her breasts nicely. All we're saying is maximize your assets, but do it tastefully.

Hip Tip   *According to The Breast Site, "70 percent of women wear the wrong size and style of bra." We women should get measured every three to six months since our bodies are always changing. Next time you're out shopping for a new bra, ask a sales clerk to measure you. Employees at most stores like Victoria's Secret and Gap Body are trained to assist you. Or grab a measuring tape and do it yourself. Check out www.thebreastsite.com for tips and advice for finding your perfect size.*

◆ **Camouflage your flaws.** So you haven't learned to love your hips yet. And of course you hate the mole above your upper lip (even though Cindy Crawford made millions from hers). In a perfect world, we'd love our bodies and our looks. But as we all know, a holiday season full of candy corn, pumpkin pie or Kris Kringle cookies can do in our bodies for months. So no matter that you've been blessed with a booty that makes buying jeans and bikinis nothing short of hell, it's important to love yourself no matter how you look. But we'll keep it real with you and offer this bit of advice: Downplay the parts of your appearance that you aren't as proud of and play up the features you love. It'll boost your ego and help you walk with pride.

◆ **Wear a smile.** Your best accessory can't be purchased. It's the genuine happiness you exude that makes people want to be near you. Be genuinely happy at the office and show it with a smile. Of course, like material accessories, you don't want to overdo it. Don't be Miss Annoying Bubbly or Giggly Girl. Your colleagues will grow to hate you for it. After all, being real includes having real-life ups and downs.

Hip Tip *Spare your clients and colleagues from smelling and seeing your business-lunch leftovers. Keep a thin pack of breath mints and a travel-size container of dental floss (both of which run between $1 and $2 at a drug store) stashed in your purse. Excuse yourself from the table after you finish eating to upkeep your brilliant smile. Also, store an extra toothbrush and a small tube of mint-fresh toothpaste in a plastic baggie in your desk drawer (both cost a little over $1 at a drugstore), to give your smile and breath some midday lovin'. Your cubicle mate and dentist will thank you for it. Just be extra careful not to slop toothpaste on your outfit.*

◆ **Make confidence your uniform.** Despite all the exterior layers of fabric, nothing can hide your confidence level (or lack thereof) from your public. So when you know your stuff, don't be afraid to walk and speak with certainty. And if you don't feel confident, fake it! Like a good pair of faux diamond earrings, pretending to be confident when you're not really feeling it can look just as appealing as the real deal. Just don't get cocky and become a know-it-all. If you ain't got the goods for your boss or client at the moment, perhaps you should admit it. Your belief in yourself and your ability to get the job done to their satisfaction is what's most important. Try, "John, I'm not quite sure why that is, but I'll look into it and get that information to you by tomorrow." Whatever you do, don't offer excuses about why you can't get the information or that you were never told you needed it. Have a can-do attitude and just make it happen to the best of your ability.

—⚬⚬⚬—

Have fun with your work wardrobe — because if you look good, you'll feel good and it'll show. And if there's a day you're not feeling it, let your clothes fake it for you!

Pretty In Pink:
Brushing Up on Your Work Hair and Make-up

—❦❦—

"In my world, my hairstyle is a representation of my work and how I feel about myself. It's also directly related to my profits. If I appear disheveled or sport an outdated, unkempt hairstyle, why should a client trust me to create a look for her that is brilliant? So even if I'm not feeling my best one day, I'll go for the low-maintenance, but fashionably coiffed look. You'd be surprised at how just a little lipstick and a neatly pulled-back 'do' will make people feel like they can trust you!"

—Sandra, 33, Hair Stylist and Instructor

Hair and make-up should be a wardrobe accessory, like a good pair of shoes or handbag. How you choose to style your hair and enhance your facial features (or do nothing to highlight your outer beauty) almost says more than your work experience for making sound judgment calls. While your hair and make-up aren't likely going to get you a job, they could be a factor in why you don't get a position or why a client doesn't sign with you.

A Hair-y Situation

Remember when you were 15 years old and spent hours diligently perfecting your trendy coif? Now that you've got a bit more going on in your life (say kids, job, husband or education), your haircut and style needs — and the time you put into them — have likely changed drastically since adolescence. (And thank goodness, 'cuz looking back, those big bouffant bangs never looked good on any of us!) But how do you know which cut and style is good for you and fits your office grooming etiquette? Consider a few of the factors below so your outer appearance doesn't interfere with your rise from department assistant to president.

◆ **Pick a haircut and style** that balances your personality with your office climate. Like lipstick and eyeliner punch up your face, a good haircut and style can speak volumes about your personality or mood. Maybe you're a wild girl within, but your day job as an accountant or attorney isn't conducive to an edgy runway Mohawk. If that's the case, opt for a cut that's versatile. Your weekday hair can be corporate-friendly and conservative. But when the weekend rolls around, style it to reveal the racy pink streak hidden beneath your long locks. Be true to you. That's important. But so is paying your bills. So when deciding how to cut your hair, consider the attention — good or bad — it may cause you at work.

◆ **Get a cut that enhances your face shape** and hair texture. Sure, you may love Jennifer Anniston's extra long and straight hair-do, or Gwen Stephani's ever-changing rock-star mop, but the same haircut and style may not be the best look for you. (Besides, having their hairstyle doesn't mean you're going to get their wealth, love lives or insane fame.) If you really must have the haircut of Hollywood's biggest starlets (or homecoming queen from your university), take a page from their stylebook and ask your professional stylist to personalize it to fit your face shape and hair texture. Trust us: Infusing their cut into a style that compliments your facial features will look better than your trying to be someone you ain't.

◆ **Get a cut and style that reflects your lifestyle.** You hate the mornings and you're always running late. If getting the kids ready for school or the traffic often sets you behind (or your late-night party time makes rolling out of bed a chore), don't add to your tardiness by getting a cut and style that takes serious time to tame. Or perhaps you drive a convertible and need hair that works with the wind-blown look, or you live in a humid climate and your hair is prone to frizz. Whatever your situation, make sure you get a cut that you can work into your everyday needs. Be realistic. Don't build a life around your hairstyle. Let your hairstyle enhance your life.

gather it into a low-side ponytail and wrap it into an off-center bun. It'll shift the focus to your facial features and attire while your hair will still looked coifed. Then dab on vibrant red lip-gloss as you pull out of your driveway or apply a little blush to rosy up your striking cheekbones. It'll brighten your look, lift your spirits and give the appearance that you're pulled together even if you're not.

◆ **Change your hairstyle as you mature.** That doesn't necessarily mean you have to crop your 'do as you approach your late 20s and mid-30s. Age-appropriate haircuts are becoming less defined. What's a good rule of thumb for hairstyles in the workplace as you grow older? Wear what's appropriate for your workplace, a style that stays out of your way while you work and a look that compliments your face and overall style (because it's bound to have changed too, thank goodness). Check out mainstream magazines, catalogs and newspaper ads that are targeted for your specific age and region. Also, consult a professional for a look that meets all your needs.

Hip Tip   *If you're in your 20s and on the younger side for your office, you may want a look that's more mature, but not stodgy. To accomplish this, select a classic cut like a "bob." Do not cut bangs, which will make you look younger. Your hair color should be clean and simple with natural-looking highlights (skip those chunky streaks). If you're in your mid-30s, consider cutting bangs. They'll take years away from your face. Chunky streaks, tastefully done, can make you look fashionable without appearing like you're trying to relive your youth.*

◆ **Use modern advances moderately to amplify your hair attraction.** Weaves, hair extensions and wigs serve various purposes and offer instant, new looks, and today's advances in au natural hair can oftentimes go undetected by others. Weaves and hair extensions can add a little volume to fine hair or hair loss, or heck, maybe you just want to try a little something different. Whatever your reason for wanting to add hair you weren't born with or have lost, investigate your options thoroughly before dropping a dime. This is not a place to skimp. Invest in a piece that blends well with what you've got. A bad weave, extension or wig can actually make your appearance worse. Consult a professional and take a friend with you whom you know you can trust to tell you the truth.

◆ **Pick a color that accents your skin tone.** Whether you're naturally a redhead, blonde or brunette, in a conservative work environment, sporting a color that looks like you were born with it (despite that you paid $100 to get it) is best. But, if you're a beautician, student, rock star or fashion commentator, doing something a bit more dramatic — like sporting the new hair trend before it hits the streets — can work in your favor. Bottom line, read your "office etiquette" before dyeing your hair a drastic color. In a more conservative climate, play it safe at work by making a subtle color change over time. And most important, girl, tend to those roots! Because even the incredible beauty of a rose is hard to see in a garden overgrown with weeds.

Hip Tip *Skip the at-home highlight kits. See a professional for a hair color consultation and procedure. Highlighting your own rarely turns out well. But if you insist on coloring your own hair because you're opting for a color that's not too far from what God gave you, do yourself a favor and don't dye your skin in the process. Grab some lip balm or petroleum jelly. By simply rubbing some along your hairline, you'll avoid dyeing your skin while transforming your tresses.*

◆ **Do you or don't you do hair chemical treatments?** Chemical treatments offer insight as to whether the grass is really greener on the other side. But neither straight nor curly hair is a "one style fits all." Again, here's a situation where you'll want to consult your beautician for what works best for your features and lifestyle.

◆ **Style your 'do with diligence.** Now that you've taken great care in finding the perfect cut and color for you and your career, the critical element becomes styling it in a manner that says what you need it to.

☐ Use products, but don't over-produce. Too much of anything — gel, hairspray, grease, pomade — doesn't look or feel good!

HipTip *Always apply conditioner from the ears down. Avoid conditioning your scalp. It can weigh down hair or make it appear greasy, instead of soft and luscious.*

☐ Pull it back. A low, slicked-back ponytail, twist or bun, with or without tamely coifed bangs, offers an easy and conservative-professional look at the office, in the courtroom or for a job interview.

☐ Save the pigtails or braids for the weekends or for going out, unless, of course, you work as a sales clerk at the ever-trendy Forever 21 clothing store. This look gives a more playful and youthful appearance; not exactly the qualities fitting a flight attendant, stockbroker or teacher whose clients are entrusting them with their most precious commodities.

☐ Pull the top and sides of your hair back into a low, loose pin while letting the lower half lay long. This style is a good, safe compromise for liberating your conservative office hair without risking a whole lot.

☐ Tame your curly or wavy hairstyle. Windblown curly and wavy hair with no taming can say you're adventurous or simply unruly. It's how you style (or don't) your curly locks that determines if you project a sassy, romantic or frazzled appearance. To achieve a more romantic look, pull it partially back as described above, letting a few curly pieces loosely shape your face. To achieve a more playful or sassy look, wear it completely down. Just make sure to manage the frizz factor with anti-frizz product (found at your beauty salon or over the counter) otherwise you'll cross the border into the frazzled territory.

Hip Tip *Static isn't just a laundry problem. To prevent static in your hair, rub a fabric-softener sheet or damp hands through your locks to neutralize any electric charge.*

☐ Straight hair at the office tends to say sophisticated sexy (and a Hip Girl knows it's all about working her every asset). But on the wrong facial structure, totally straight hair can make you look dreary and boring. In a youth-obsessed culture, that's not a look anyone should consider. Consult a professional about what looks best for your facial structure before deciding.

Hip Tip *Toss a ponytail holder in your purse, stash it in your desk drawer or wear it discreetly around your wrist to quickly pull your hair back into a sleek and low ponytail or bun.*

☐ Stylishly short and pixie-cropped hairstyles are equally work-safe sexy (not to mention usually less time-consuming). If you've got the features and the confidence to carry this look off, like Halle Berry, Mandy Moore or Sharon Stone, props to you! Go for it!

☐ Tame your bangs at work. The Big Bang theory doesn't apply here. Save that look for your weekend runway modeling gig. As we mentioned earlier, bangs make a woman look younger. What's the bottom line with bangs in the workplace? If you look good in them, they are age-appropriate and you wear them in a natural manner, go for it, girl. On the right face, bangs can look attractive and offer a simple alternative to spice up your typical hairstyle.

◆ **Maintain your mop.** Get your hair trimmed regularly (every four to six weeks, sometimes a little more or less). Cut off the dead, split ends. Keep your look ever-modern. Wash it regularly and comb it. Nourish it with oil treatments or conditioner to keep it looking healthy. Color it when roots start showing. Okay, we know we're starting to sound like your mother. But all we're saying, girl, is take care of your overall appearance (and leave the fun, dirty-gritty look for weekends.)

◆ **Accessorize hair maturely.** Hats, rubber bands with decorations, barrettes, chopsticks, scarves, headbands and designer bobby pins can be a perfect way to top off your overall look. Wear hair accessories that compliment your overall outfit and age. Take into consideration your overall fashion statement before adding a hair accessory. These simple additions can quickly turn into tacky and over-the-top distractions.

◆ **Hands-free hairdo.** It's a simple suggestion, but easy to break: Keep your hands out of your hair at work. Yep, that means save the flirtatious hair twirling and flipping for the bars. In the office, that kind of overt seduction is potential trouble. And if you catch yourself running your fingers through your hair or twirling it as a matter of habit, pull it back. You lose credibility with and the attention of your audience. Whether you're instructing kids to focus or attempting to sell your peers on your ideas, fidgeting with your hair or hair accessories is distracting to you and others.

Make-up Tips 101

Have you ever wished you knew all the secrets of a professional make-up artist? We consulted professionals to the stars from Hollywood's most prestigious beauty and day spa, Fred Seagal Beauty. Below are their top 10 trade secrets to punch up your work make-up.

1. **Can't make it home to freshen up** between your day gig and last-minute after-hours drink meeting? Forgo trying to stuff a cumbersome make-up bag into your evening bag. All you need are some tissues, lip balm, facial mist and a stick of creamy blush. To freshen up your look on the run, remove the day's worth of dust and dirt by gently wiping your face with a soft, clean, dry tissue. Then smooth all your make-up out with your fingers, especially blending in excess eye shadow creases. Next, comb through your eyelashes and shape your eyebrows with your fingers. Then, refresh your skin with a spritz of facial water or a rosemary mist. (Try Shu Uemura Facial Mist, Aveda, M.A.C's Fix + or Kiehls, found in department stores, salons, beauty supply stores or on-line.) Let it dry naturally; don't rub it in. Whatever you do, don't pile more make-up on top of the day's leftovers. More is not the solution here. Instead, use a good cream blush or a one-piece-meets-all-needs stick and apply a little on your cheeks, under your eyebrows and a hint on your lips. Shisedo Rose Grimpante is a good multi-purpose cream blush, as well as

Smashbox or Nars who offer plenty of choices, and can be found in department stores, on-line or select beauty spas. If you don't have a creamy blush, your good ol' trusty lipstick will do the trick just as well. Voila! You'll look as good as new.

HipTip Apply your concealer and powder onto clean lips prior to lining and applying your lipstick and gloss in the morning. This will help your lipstick last longer throughout the day.

2. **Make your make-up style appropriate** to your various work functions. Generally, day make-up should reflect a clean beauty: groomed, not dewy, well-blended, more neutral in color range and with a matte finish. In an especially conservative work environment, don't use vibrant lipsticks or eye shadows. If you want to rock the boardroom with your power red lipstick, select a deeper red, like burgundy, with a matte finish. Cocktail party make-up can show-off your flair for fun with more shiny make-up styles, smoky eyes and fake eyelashes.

HipTip Want to know the skinny of all your favorite beauty products? Check out Paula Begoun's book Don't Go to the Cosmetics Counter Without Me. This product-by-product guide gives detailed reviews for everything from facial cleansers and moisturizers to eye shadows and lipsticks. Careful, it may just change how you shop.

3. **Focus on one facial feature at a time.** Don't enhance your eyes with aquamarine shadow, red lips and pink blush all at once. That's a whole lot going on. To play up your lips with power red, go barely there on your eyes and cheekbones. Conversely, if you want your

eyes to pop with color or you want to wear the smoky, sex-pot appearance (for those after-hours get-togethers), choose a natural-colored lip-gloss.

4. **Choose your make-up** based on your skin tone, facial features and work climate, not your day's outfit. Find your image and define your style: Who you are, how you want to represent yourself with others. Then play around with it, varying ever so slightly from your core appearance.

5. **Practice good make-up grooming maintenance.** Shape your eyebrows because they liven up your whole look. If you can swing it financially, get them professionally done, either waxed or plucked (which runs between $15 and $30). Change your make-up foundation when your skin condition or skin color changes (like in winter when it becomes more dry and pale, or in summer when your beach brown tan turns a bit oily). Moisturize your skin at least twice a day and frost your face with a mist.

6. **Not one for make-up,** but want to look refreshed and coiffed 24/7? Get your eyelashes tinted. (Prices range from $10 to $20.) The process takes approximately 15 minutes and lasts for about four to six weeks. Keep your lips glossy with your favorite lip balm.

7. **Coordinate color palettes** from head-to-toe. We suggest a few coordinates to play up brown-toned outfits, using the most important make-up factors — your skin tone and which features you want to enhance or hide.

   ☐ Deep brown dress (based in yellow or orange) + olive skin = orange-based make-up complimented by neutral, warm colors.

   ☐ Deep brown dress + pink-based skin = pink-based make-up like fuchsia or mauve.

☐ Deep brown dress (based in charcoal) + pink-based skin = baby blue eyes, light pink, glossy lips and raised cheekbones.

Hip Tip *If you'd like assistance figuring out which make-up colors best suit you but you dread shopping in department stores, help is just a click away. Hop onto your computer and log onto www.covergirl.com. After answering just a few questions, you'll be given a list of Cover Girl's products and colors that are geared toward you. If you need more of a personal touch, they have on-line consultants to help assist you. Best of all, you can order the products right from their site or pick them up at any drugstore. Now that's convenient!*

8. **Fight office shine.** Start in the morning with a mattifying, oil-free under-base lotion. Then apply the foundation or powder that fits your skin type and the rest of your make-up. Dayside, use make-up blotters to dissipate shine. Mac make-up blotters are good for skin that gets shiny; Shisedo make-up blotters are better for oily skin types. If you don't have a make-up blotter at your disposal, use a tissue. Press the tissue against your forehead and chin. Blot, don't wipe. Add more powder if you must. Just dust a brush with powder and apply for a softer, more blended appearance.

Hip Tip *Applying lipstick or other make-up at work should be done discreetly. Do it in the ladies room or with your office door closed. If you're out to lunch with a client, excuse yourself first from the table to blot your shine away. Re-application of make-up in front of co-workers, bosses or clients is distracting and tacky.*

9. **Pick a scent,** but don't become the scent. Perfume punches up your overall presentation. Select one or two signature fragrances. Just

make sure not to drench yourself in it. Either put a little on your finger and dab it on two or three different parts of your body, or spritz a bit in the air and walk into it. You should wear the perfume. It shouldn't resonate long after you've left.

10. **Nail your Hip Girl look.** Nothing looks worse than a badly chipped bright pink manicure, especially in a conservative work environment. Stash a packet of on-the-go nail polish remover pads in your purse or glove box. (Your local pharmacy usually sells travel packets of Cutex or other brands for $2 to $3). Then quickly coat your nails with Express drying clear nail polish for a clean, coiffed appearance (because no one needs to know you could barely pull yourself out of bed this morning). The nail polish remover pads are also great for removing evidence of your weekend of partying. When good ol'-fashioned soap and water won't dissolve the bar stamp from your wrist, the nail polish remover pad will. If you don't have time to change your nail polish during the workweek to compliment your office outfit, opt for a versatile look that will last all week long, like a ballet slipper colored hue or a classic French manicure. Lastly, keep a nail file in your purse or top drawer of your desk to keep all your nails even in length, even in emergency situations. A Hip Girl is always prepared to handle disasters with style and grace.

Make your office hair and make-up an asset, not a distraction. Your co-workers should want to emulate your look, not make fun of it.

PART TWO

Gettin' Jiggy on the Job

A re you stuck in a rut at your job or crossing your fingers that your nosey little office-mate gets transferred, oh, across continents? Are you tied up in knots over the office hottie who was clearly flirting with you at the Christmas party? Just like when we were in kindergarten and we'd color outside the lines, defining and staying within the perimeters of what's professional is difficult when our hearts, instincts and hormones shade our judgment of appropriate behavior in the workplace. Read on to learn the tenuous life lessons neither your Girl Scout Handbook nor your college education taught you.

Smart & Savvy Strategies for Success:

Six Simple Tactics for Managing Workplace Politics

———∞∞∞———

"After college, I worked as a personal trainer before switching to recruiting employees in the automotive industry. Now I work as a bartender to pursue my career as an actress. Ironically, it's my talent for being a 'people person' that's made me successful in each field. Whether a client is paying me to whip their body into shape, pour them a good drink or find a star employee, I make more money if I'm in tune with their subliminal needs for good conversation, motivation or just a trusty ear for listening."

—Stella, 28, Aspiring Actress/Bartender

A college education gives you the foundation for your specific trade or profession. We Hip Girls are here to help where the classroom instruction leaves off. Employers expect you to already be skilled at the fundamentals of your field. But professors rarely cover the intangible job tactics required to survive and succeed in your career. Regardless of your college experience, every Hip Girl knows that hard work, productivity and good references aren't enough to get the job, the promotion or the corner office with a window. Nope. Most of those benefits are based on your ability to successfully navigate through office politics and protocol. So roll up your sleeves and get ready to shovel. It's your ability to foresee and deal with the "dirty" work that'll take you where you want to go.

Read Body Language

This might be the most important trait you pick up as an employee, employer or a business owner. Being able to gauge your co-worker, client, subordinate, audience or boss's bodily cues gives you an advantage in getting what you want or managing a situation before it becomes a problem. Below are some cues regarding when you should or shouldn't persist in addressing such things as the meeting's notes with your boss, an issue with the judge, the passenger's behavior with the steward or the purchase of a new computer for your home office with your husband.

◆ **Are they body busy?** Intense phone conversations, managing jumping and screaming children, computer zoning and frantic typing are obvious signs the person is involved somewhere else. If the attention of the person you need is clearly focused elsewhere, wait to communicate with him or her when he or she can be present with you. If it's an emergency, say so.

Hip Tip *Look busy yourself, even if you're just masking a quick call from a friend. Despite seeing that you're productive and efficient at your job, employers need to feel like they're getting every second of your time when you're on their dime. Never let 'em catch you standing and zoning out, sitting down on a job that requires standing, overly chatting with your cubicle mate, sleeping on the plane trip (especially while they're slaving away) or freshening up your make-up. Sit or stand straight, and look alert while on the job. Don't put your feet up on the desk or sleep in the office, even if you think everyone's gone home (you never know who might be lingering in the halls). And, whenever possible, no matter how busy you really may be, do your best to make yourself available to co-workers when they need you during the work day.*

◆ **Are they subliminally out of it?** Some distractions are not necessarily so overt. Distractions come in all sizes, shapes and colors. (Have you ever tried talking to your guy during a football game? Girl, you might as well give up on that one.) They may even be invisible, like emotional distractions. Does your colleague usually come in full make-up and trendy fashions, yet today is barely wearing a drop of make-up, has her hair pulled back and is dressed casually? She may not be feeling well, or she may have her mind on something more pressing. Hearing about your fun-filled weekend in the Hamptons with your new boyfriend may not be time appropriate. Other subliminal signs include illness cues (coughing, sneezing, constant nose-blowing, watery-eyes or hunched-over posture), little conversation or a closed door (particularly if your co-worker, employee, boss or client is a usual jabber mouth), and answers or comments that don't seem to address the issue at hand or are brief and meant to quickly dismiss.

Hip Tip *Verbal communication is the most obvious cue about when to discuss important matters. Don't dismiss clear verbal signs by hearing what you want to hear, instead of what is being said. And if you don't understand what your boss, colleague or client is saying, then say so and ask for clarity. Guessing, analyzing or assuming information can often lead to misunderstandings.*

◆ **Play the match game.** Pair verbal cues with body cues. Does your boss say you're not interrupting anything, but her body language says something opposite — like she's looking out the window, at the clock or at her caller ID when the phone rings? Does your co-worker say no, she doesn't need your help, but you overhear her complaining to a friend or you see her struggling with the copy machine for an hour? Sometimes, both in our personal and professional lives, we don't say exactly what we mean. Being able to discern what your co-worker needs no matter what she says will mean the world to the person whose attention you need. If possible, wait to speak with them on their timeframe.

Approach is Everything

Remember when your mom taught you, "If you can't say something nice, don't say anything all"? Well, mom was right. Positioning a request, comment, question or answer appropriately in any situation is imperative to successful communication. It's the biggest factor in determining if you'll get the information you need, can resolve a dispute or keep one from igniting, or if you'll get the work done for you. For instance, you might laugh if your husband demands you cook dinner for him and his friends. But if he approaches you with a hug and kiss and asks if you wouldn't mind making your famous, delicious dish, you'd be flattered. Check out some ways below to help you better communicate in your workplace.

◆ **First, consistently show you genuinely care** about your co-worker, client, employee or boss. Say, "Hello, how are you?" and wait for a reply. That small gesture will mean a ton. You can take it a step further and inquire about what they did over the weekend or if they have big plans for vacation. Other simple efforts include occasionally surprising them with bagels or coffee, a flower to brighten their day or, if you're in charge, letting them go home early or randomly giving them the day off.

◆**Make employers, employees and clients feel valued and important.** You can do this by encouraging and respecting their opinions. Whether you're the decision-maker, colleague or worker-bee, empower your subordinates, office-mate or boss by encouraging and enabling them to vocalize their ideas. But don't stop there. Show them you hear what they're saying. Make every effort to reinforce their comments positively, either by finding a way to make their idea work or reassuring them that their idea is good, but giving them solid reasons why it won't work this time.

◆ **Ask, don't tell.** Which would you rather hear or read:

☐ Can you fax these papers for me?
☐ Please fax these papers for me!
☐ I need these papers faxed.

While each sentence clearly says what you need, the second and third versions are more forceful and direct. If you're dealing with a child or unruly subordinate, you may need to be more direct and use the second or third version. But overall, we suggest you opt for the first version because we all just want to feel valued and respected. So whether you're in charge, a client, a subordinate or a customer, get your needs met with less attitude and hassle by asking for assistance in a way that is not off-putting to the receiver.

◆ **Build team spirit** by making people feel authentically needed and responsible. Use a group project or event as an opportunity to delegate responsibility to cohorts. Using the word "we" when appropriate can help lay the foundation for a group-inspired accomplishment. For example: "We should start thinking about how we're going to market the new product." Follow up with how we'll work together to make it happen. For example: "Can you make a list of people we should invite? I'll investigate venues for us to hold the party." And, most importantly, follow the team spirit through by giving props to the people who served as your support system for success.

◆ **Use respect to fight potential fires.** So you weren't so savvy about calling your sorority sister out on the table in front of her family for borrowing your favorite top without permission. Well, now that you're a Hip Girl, you recognize that how and when you approach someone about sticky situations makes all the difference in your long-term relationship. If you absolutely cannot find a way to help a co-worker, boss, subordinate or client in need, or you are the recipient of a disrespectful comment or behavior, take the high road and be polite but firm about standing up for yourself. When you reply, offer solid reasons why you can't help and offer possible options. Sometimes being right isn't as important as getting the job done. In some cases, you'll be more respected for your ability to work out problems. Check out a couple of scenarios below for how to respectfully combat office fires.

Situation 1: Sally, a same-level colleague, says something or emails you in a tone that sounds as if she's your boss: "From now on, you should write your weekly report in a more efficient format, like this one." You are fuming! Just who does she think she is, your boss? That won't fly with you. Now take a second here to recognize that what you do next could make or break your name with co-workers and bosses. You:

- ☐ Take a deep breath and collect your thoughts and contain your emotions before responding. Jot down bullet points, if necessary, to identify your main concerns.
- ☐ Recognize that returning the disrespectful tone will only create a bigger problem.
- ☐ Calmly respond: "Your chart seems very efficient and I'm glad it works for you. My direct report, however, has not asked me to change my format style. I'll happily mention your concerns, however."
- ☐ Decide if you should inform your boss about the dispute. *(See Picking and Choosing Your Battles.)*
- ☐ If you feel you should tell your boss, provide her with just the facts of the story.
- ☐ If the attack happened via email, forward all communication to your boss and write: "Please see Susan's concerns below about my weekly reports. How would you like me to handle this?"
- ☐ If you don't have documentation, perhaps you mention it in your private, weekly update with your boss. (Because the last thing you want to do is make it a bigger deal than it is. Otherwise, you'll come across as a crybaby. And that's the first sign of a Hip Girl imposter.) As you conclude your weekly meeting, say: "So, Susan

mentioned to me earlier this week that she was concerned about the format for my weekly notes. Are you satisfied with them, or is there another way you'd like me to submit them? And how would you like to let Susan know your wishes?" Any good boss will take the bait and resolve Susan's inappropriate, bossy behavior promptly and respectfully.

Situation 2: Your boss asks you to travel over the weekend at the last minute to cover a photo shoot for her. You've already made plans. You make every attempt to cancel them to accommodate your boss's request, but to no avail. You:

☐　Ask to speak with your boss in private.

☐　Consider saying, "I really appreciate the opportunity to cover the shoot this weekend. I tried to postpone my weekend plans to accommodate your request, but I couldn't get a refund for my ski getaway. I'm sorry, but I won't be able to cover the shoot this weekend. Can you ask John to handle it instead?"

☐　Your boss says no. Now you must decide if losing the money from your planned trip and upsetting your kids is the lesser of two evils.

☐　If you decide to stick to your guns, you still might be able to hold your own and get your way. Use your history of accommodating her to see it from your perspective. Be specific and say something like: "Well, I covered the last-minute shoot in Texas two weeks ago, the client meeting a month ago for Kevin and I'm happily covering the shoot in Japan next weekend. I feel strongly that I consistently go above and beyond to show my loyalty to you and the company and would really appreciate your understanding on this matter."

☐　If that doesn't work, then it's up to you to decide if acquiescing or standing firm is worth the repercussions.

◆ **Manage expectations from the get-go** by using language that softens the blow. Most of the time you're better off telling your boss, client or office-mates as soon as you're aware of challenges (like unrealistic deadlines, logistical issues or workload problems) and potential crisis situations (your staff called in sick, your client refuses to do the television interview or the budget is missing $100,000. YIKES!). Informing the appropriate supervisor, client and comrades about problematic situations covers your behind. But do it in a way that shows them if anyone can get the job done or resolve a problem, it's you. Check out a couple approaches below:

◻ A teacher managing her student's parent: "I realize you had family visiting during this week, but your child consistently failed to turn in many of her homework assignments over the past few months. I really need your support enforcing the importance of getting her homework turned in so she doesn't fall behind and to prepare your daughter for middle school."

◻ A physical therapist managing a demanding patient: "I really appreciate that you trust and value my work so much. But I need you to understand that your bad back will not get better if you don't do your daily exercises on your own at home too."

◻ A businesswoman managing her boss: "I'm thrilled to be working on this account. As you know, I'm also currently working on two others. They end in December. Therefore, I believe I can get started on the new account on January 1."

◆ **Have a can-do demeanor.** People are attracted to an optimistic attitude. Promise realistic results, and work hard to deliver the goods.

◆ **Fake it 'til you make it.** So you don't know how to run the copy machine or, even though you're a certified real estate agent, you haven't sold a home yet. That doesn't mean you're not up to the challenge. A Hip Girl is resourceful and will figure it out as she goes along. As long as you meet the legal standards and obligations, projecting an image of confidence and experience is on the up-n-up. And if you decide to divulge your inexperience, make sure to back it with confidence in your abilities to make it happen.

Pick & Choose Your Battles

As a country, we pick and choose battles on a daily basis. If we didn't, we'd find ourselves embroiled in global disputes far more often. Okay, so you're not into international relations. Encourage a peace treaty in your own home and office by incorporating this effort more often. (Any happily married Hip Girl will attest: Occasionally overlooking her husband's housekeeping habits may serve her interests best overall.)

◆ **First, evaluate how important the subject is to you.** Was getting the interior instead of the corner office detrimental to you? Was getting Christmas off imperative to your family's well-being? If not, perhaps this disappointment is better left unmentioned until it can be used as an example in another battle worth fighting.

◆ **What are the possible repercussions if you speak up?**

◆ **What are the possible repercussions if you don't speak up?**

◆ **Don't keep score, keep note.** If you decide to keep this one under wraps, make a mental note in case you need to pull it out as a trump card when it matters more.

◆ **If you decide a battle is worth fighting,** be smart about your approach. Revisit the Approach is Everything section before you delve in.

Respect the Chain of Command

Okay, so it wasn't fair when your older brother or sister got to ride shotgun just because they were born before you. Or how about when the seniors got to choose where the freshman sat in the cafeteria? Either way, you had to respect their authority and try not to get around it by tattling to your parents or teacher. Those same rules apply as an adult in the workplace.

◆ **Whether you have a problem, question or concern,** you should almost always address it directly with the person you're dealing with first.

Hip Tip *Don't engage in an argument via email. If you anticipate a disagreement, discuss it in person or over the phone. Emails can be easily misinterpreted and turn a spark into a fire. They can also serve as documentation that could work against you.*

◆ **If you can't resolve the issue,** discuss the issue with your direct report.

◆ **If you don't get an answer** — or you get an answer you don't like — follow up with your direct report again. Figure out if this is a time to suck it up and move on.

◆ **If all your efforts to get what you need have failed,** your final option might be to take it to a higher court. Usurping your boss by going to her boss, human resources, the union or the equalitarian organization is a risky move. Make sure the matter is of high importance to you. Be clear about your intentions. These are high stakes you're playing for. Your motivation shouldn't be vindictive, but done out of fairness and principle. Keep in mind some decisions aren't fair and you'll just have to live with them, just like when you were younger and knew it wasn't your turn to wash the dishes.

Find and Be an Everyday Mentor

Rarely is anyone innately omnipotent at his or her job. Years of mistakes and successes were required to get where they are. So don't overestimate the power of your talent and knowledge, because even though you're good at what you do, there's always someone better. Instead of secretly envying their success, strive to be their friend so you can learn from them.

◆ **Pick a mentor you can access.** Many of us idolize athletes like Jackie Joyner Kersey or Tara Lipinski, or popular stars like Reese Witherspoon, Julia Roberts or Oprah Winfrey. While these role models serve their larger-than-life purposes, picking a Hip Girl or Cool Guy who's within reach makes seeking advice much easier. Look to an influential teacher, coach, boss, colleague, client, alumni, association member or friend to model your work style after.

Hip Tip *Remember, a mentor is not your best friend or a love interest. If your mentor falls into one of these categories, it's time to find yourself someone new to look up to.*

◆ **Choose a mentor who wants to be your champion.** You may be impressed by your boss's career success, but what's he worth to you if he's not willing to help with your career through guidance, acknowledgements or networking?

◆ **Approach your mentor-candidate professionally.** So you've found someone you think suits your mentor needs. How should you proceed? If you already have an established working relationship, sometimes the mentoring process develops naturally. In this situation, you may not need to verbally define mentorship ground rules; you merely need to be present and active in the give-and-take needs of your relationship. In other situations, you will need to be more forthright in approaching a mentor and designing a mentoring structure. We suggest you check with your HR department to see if they have a program that will make approaching your mentor candidate easier. If not, make a point to be where you may "rub elbows" with your mentor candidate, such as an industry event, a meeting or a company party. Find an appropriate time to pull that person aside (not when everyone else is swarming and fighting for her time) and introduce yourself. Ask if you can take her to lunch or schedule an appointment to talk about her successes. Prepare for the meeting by coming up with questions about her rise in her career. Open your meeting with who you are (an assistant for Jane Paul on the third floor), followed by why you wanted to meet with her (you've admired her work from afar). Offer specific examples of where and when you were first impressed by her. This will show you've done your homework, and she will likely be flattered by your genuine interest. If the conversation feels like it's going in the right direction, now's your chance to inquire if she'd be willing to be your mentor. If she says no, say you understand, and thank her for her time. (Don't take it personally. Like in dating, just move on and find someone who can meet your needs.) If she says yes, define the mentorship program with a loose structure. Specifically, ask if she's okay meeting you bi-weekly, where she'd like to meet, how best to reach her (via email or phone) in-between meetings, and reassure her that your conversations will remain confidential. And remember that, at least at first, she's doing you a favor. Try to be as flexible to her needs and schedule as possible.

◆ **Learn by listening.** You aren't listening if you're busy talking. So when your mentor speaks, listen and absorb what she's saying. Whether you decide to take her advice or leave it, recognize the information you're receiving is invaluable.

◆ **Apply what you learn.** There's no bigger compliment to a mentor than witnessing the success of his apprentice. Thank your mentor by using what you learn from him to accomplish your own achievements.

◆ **Show loyalty.** Remember where you came from and who helped you along the way. Those are the people you should be helping and thanking on Oscar Day.

Hip Tip *Never underestimate the power of a thank you. If your mentor helped you get through a hairy situation at work or put in a good word for you, make sure you express your gratitude for her time and effort. Why not send him a personal, handwritten thank you?*

◆ **Remember, your mentor is human.** Let Wonder Woman and Jennifer Garner's character on "Alias" serve as your superhuman role models. But when dealing with your everyday hero, don't forget she is as real as you. Be prepared to forgive, support or overlook her mistakes despite her infinite knowledge, years of experience and suave demeanor. After all, no one is perfect all of the time.

Hip Tip   If your mentor's mistake is irrevocable, perhaps it's time to re-evaluate the costs and benefits of your relationship. After all, you're not bound by contract to the relationship. Just make sure to be respectful when dissolving your mentorship. There are bound to be feelings of rejection, so be careful to pull away slowly and gently.

Work Your Assets

All Hip Girls are born with talents, skills or personality characteristics to use in our careers. Identify your assets and hone them to work in your favor when pursuing your aspirations. Because working your assets is such a massive undertaking, we've devoted a whole chapter to it. Check out "Working Your Assets: Utilizing What You've Got to Get What You Want."

Take your office pulse. Then pump up your own political prowess. Just remember, your integrity is the one asset that will never fail you.

Working Your Assets:
Utilizing What You've Got to Get What You Want

———— ⌒⌒⌒ ————

"After college I knew I wanted to work in the entertainment business in some capacity, so I took a PR job that utilized my communications degree and had some entertainment clients. But I was miserable because I'm very analytical and like to work independently, and my job required intense relationship-building skills. So I networked with a then-boyfriend's contact and jumped at the opportunity to extrapolate figures and research data for a television studio. And while that boyfriend is long gone, I'm the happiest I've ever been in my career!"

—Claudia, 25, Research Analyst

Athleticism and craftsmanship are obvious talents. But not all of us have strengths that are quite so recognizable. And like a gym membership you might possess but never use, if you don't work your intangible assets, girl, then they won't do you any good. One of the most important resources you'll encounter while pursuing your career dreams is you. Yes, YOU!

Checklist of Your Assets

We are all born with or capable of honing our innate, intangible assets. Intangible assets consist of talents like street smarts, creativity, personality, aura, appearance and intelligence. Working each and every one that we possess — and learning to camouflage and accept our lack of certain others — can help us Hip Girls achieve maximum success in our careers.

What assets do you feel you bring to the table? You'll have most of them to some degree, but identify here which abilities come naturally. Take note of those you're not as strong in. It's okay; we all have room to grow. Accepting our areas of improvement will help get us where we want to go. Also, think of others not listed below, those intangible qualities your friends say they envy you for.

◆ **Personality.** Your personality is one of your most influential assets for doing well in life. So use what God gave you. You know the people who always seem to get what they want. For whatever reason, they seem to have that charm. But charm comes in various packaging. Personalities are like spices, a variety of flavors for a variety of palettes. For some, practicing a princess persona gets them places. You might be perky and outgoing like Kelly Ripa, or quirky and silly like Cameron Diaz. You might be sarcastic and witty like Joy from *The View*, who can rival with the best of the boys in the boardroom. Or you may have more of a Diane Sawyer's compassionate approach. Perhaps it's your edge like Angelina Jolie, or your smoldering and mysterious disposition like Christina Ricci, that draws others to you. Maybe it's your genuinely good heart that shines or your adventurous spirit that makes others feel alive. Whatever your dominant personality styles, recognize, accept and work them to your advantage to get what you want out of your career.

◆ **Physical Appearance.** You don't have to look like Jennifer Lopez or Halle Barry to be attractive. Just look at some runway models. They aren't all gorgeous. Most of them have at least one striking feature that stands out, like the size of their eyes, cheekbone structure or smile. Beauty truly is in the eye of the beholder. (Model Lauren Hutton, after all, worked that space between her front teeth into millions!) Not everyone loves tall, thin, blonde or tan. In fact, many of the men we talked to like curves, exotic flair or brunettes just as well. So own and hone what you've got. Physical appearance, however, will only get your foot in the door. Beyond that, it's what's below the surface that makes you worth more.

Hip Tip *If someone compliments you on your figure, project or management style, thank her. Don't be self-deprecating by finding fault with the very thing your colleague or boss is complimenting. Yet don't overdo the confidence by saying something as brazen as, "Yes, I know." Simply smile and say, "Thank you," or, if you can't stop there, add, "I work really hard at it because it's important to me," or, "Your acknowledgement and support makes it all the more meaningful."*

◆ **Intelligence.** You're a real-life rocket scientist who can regurgitate the theory of relativity off the top of your brain. Perhaps your book smarts earned you a master's degree in biochemistry, or you got average grades in school but your SAT score ruled. If your ability to grasp and extrapolate highly complicated theories, equations or statistical information can rival that of Matt Damon's character in *Good Will Hunting*, consider yourself one smart cookie. But perhaps you present yourself as clueless in matters that aren't important to you. Girl, if that's you, work it like Jessica Simpson does. While Hip Girls aren't helpless in anything we do, we're smart enough to know that sometimes other people need to feel needed and in control, too.

◆ **Street smarts.** So you're no genius; few people are. But most employers say they'd take someone with more common sense over a high IQ score. Resourcefulness, confidence, flexibility and tenacity for problem-solving are key street-smarts skills that put you in charge of your own destiny. Employers, clients, colleagues and subordinates find great comfort in the consistency of this take-charge sensibility. In fact, it's often the deciding factor for entrusting their most prized possessions — such as their kids, money and homes — to new or old reliable alliances.

◆ **Creativity.** You have a flair for being unique, an uncontrollable urge to push the limit of normalcy. You may show your creativity in such ways as your appearance, writing, party-throwing, or brainstorming sessions or hobbies, to name a few. Creativity is not a talent many people exude, so if you got it, girl, maximize it. Don't be afraid to push the envelope once in a while. Just be aware of your boss's or client's comfort level with the "different." It's a talent you might have to slowly infuse. Once you've broken the barrier, then, and only then, can you successfully bring more creativity to the job.

Hip Tip   *Be quick to thank the people who help you look good. If you're an up-and-coming movie actress whose winning style graces the pages of every fashion magazine, take the credit, but attribute some of your fashion-ista success to your stylist. If you're a magazine editor, thank your brilliant creative team for their ideas and hard work. If you're a pilot, thank your co-pilot, command center and flight attendants for making the ride smoother. Remember, you're only as good as the support team that surrounds you.*

◆ **Aura.** A Hip Girl's aura is probably the hardest of all assets to describe. It's a glow that surrounds her every day. It's that "IT" energy that's inviting in every way. For some, it's recognizable from afar. For others, their aura is felt after they've barely touched someone's heart. It's a spirit that moves, inspires, motivates or consoles you. A powerful aura is a force that may resonate only after it has left its mark. So if you're lucky enough to have a natural aura that makes others feel alive or safe, or ignites them to look within themselves, use it for good intentions and the karma will likely smile back on you.

Putting Your Assets to Work for You

◆ **Review each of the various intangible assets above** and figure out which you excel at maximizing. Are there any that would better suit your job? If so, get to honing that skill right away. If your job isn't one that can benefit from the assets you naturally bring to the table, consider pursuing an activity that can. That doesn't necessarily mean you need a new job. You may volunteer for a charity or pursue a hobby where your strengths are appreciated and utilized more.

◆ **Identify which of the intangible skills are not your strong suits.** Seek help from experts to hone those skills. You've seen it on *American Idol*: contestants who thought they had it, then Simon blatantly tells them they don't. Instead of taking his critique and learning from it, they blow him off like he's a twit. We don't think you should listen to just anyone about your skills (in fact, this Hip Girl might not have become an author if I had listened to people who questioned my writing talent). But if several people who are accredited experts in the field reinforce the same tough love, perhaps you should consider their opinions. Don't give up your dreams of being in the music business — just consider altering them a little. Maybe your path isn't as a singer, but perhaps as a songwriter or music producer.

◆ **Learn to love what you have;** learn to accept what you don't. So you weren't blessed with a so-called perfect body, or you're more of an introvert than a social charmer. Place yourself in environments that spotlight your strengths and minimize your weaknesses. For instance, if you're introverted, opt for the public relations job that requires more writing and less face-to-face contact. If your physical appearance is a clear asset, avoid a dot-com position that limits your face-to-face communication.

◆ **Be confident but humble about flaunting your assets.** Be a girl on the go. A woman with a mission. Girl-about-town with ambition. If you've got it girl, work it. But keep in mind that no one likes an arrogant, boastful co-worker. And to be honest (because that's why we're writing this book), women need to carefully display their drive and success differently than men. Otherwise, we risk intimidating the men and alienating the other women in the office. Unfortunately, that old double standard often holds true: Applaud a man for his prowess, but a Hip Girl has to carefully balance her pride and confidence with humility. Achieving this balance will rally the troops in your support.

Hip Tip *Share your wealth. Offer insight to a colleague, client or customer about how to acquire the assets they admire in you. Does she like your hair? Refer her to your stylist. Does he aspire to be an author, too? Offer him tips or details about how you got your first book deal.*

—⊸≡∭ᒲᒥ∭≡⊷—

Work your assets and camouflage your flaws. It's a key ingredient that gives a Hip Girl an edge over her competition.

You Talkin' to Me?
Etiquette for the Electronic Era

"I offered to pass my work flirt's résumé along to some colleagues in a different department. Unknowingly my email had also accidentally forwarded our little naughty exchange about what color of underwear we were wearing that day. I was mortified and panic stricken! Thank God for the 'recall' function which just barely saved me from becoming a laughing stock of all my colleagues or worse yet, fired!"

— Michelle, 25, Law School Student
and Part-time Assistant at a Law Firm

Face-time with clients, colleagues, boss or customers is invaluable for building and maintaining your business relationships. But if trans-continental traveling isn't in your budget, today's modern world offers a wealth of technology with which to exchange information with your start-up clothing manufacturer in China. Since communicating electronically and digitally has become more prevalent than the archaic method of reaching out and touching someone via the yellow pages, knowing how to properly correspond will help alleviate misunderstandings and giant misperceptions about your intentions and interest.

Dial-up Do's and Don'ts

Today's technologically advanced age makes multi-tasking easier by improving productivity and efficiency. But substituting voices or text for in-person meet-n-greets comes with unwritten etiquette. Below are some top tips to consider for the technologically savvy sister to consider when building business relationships in the electronic era.

Do . . .

◆ **Use landlines whenever possible to ensure a quality connection.** Nothing is more frustrating than dropping a four-person conference call because someone's background traffic noise makes the others inaudible. Or worse, you get nothing but static as you're about to be connected for your very important interview with your potential East Coast employer.

◆ **Use cell phones to keep you connected while you're motoring.** When you're taking fifth-graders on an overnight trip to the wilderness and one gets homesick, if all else fails, dial up his mom and dad to console him.

◆ **Use text messaging for a quick, non-disruptive way** to exchange simple information with someone you know very well. The letters that you can electronically transmit from your cell phone or Blackberry create your text message. You punch them in according to their number pairings on your electronic gadget. Simple "yes" or "no" responses or one-sentence requests are great for communicating via text messaging. For instance, text message your assistant, "Can you email me directions to the Roosevelt Hotel?," or your boss, "I'll be there in 5" for the meeting already in progress.

Hip Tip *Travel often? Invest in an additional charger for your cell phone. Just leave it in your suitcase and you'll never have to worry about your battery dying while you're away from home again. Also, check with your service provider (you know, the people you cut your monthly cell phone check to) to see if your phone will work in a different state or country. Select the system (digital, analog, dual-mode or GSM) and phone that best suits your individual business needs.*

◆ **Take your personal assistant with you.** Cellular phones and PDAs (personal digital assistants) are one-stop-shopping for keeping your life organized, checking your flight status on the Internet, remembering contact information or reporting back to your boss about the latest fall looks in Milan via email, text messaging and/or picture-taking.

Hip Tip *Wish your cell phone could do more? Log on to major wireless carriers — like Verizonwireless.com, AT&Twireless.com or Cingular.com. They offer many options in PDAs. You can opt for a handheld or palm-sized device like the ever-popular Blackberry or Sidekick, depending on your need for size and function. PDAs combine the function of your cell phone with that of your personal computer. Now you can surf the Net, send emails, keep a to-do list, manage expense reports and talk to your clients all on the same device.*

Check your local wireless carrier for more information by looking in the yellow pages under "cellular companies." Or you can punch in key words "cellular companies" in a search engine on your computer accompanied by "&" and your state or city, or by logging on to the Websites of the various major wireless carries mentioned above to locate a store near you.

◆ **Let voicemail take your incoming call** if you're online with your boss or client (unless, of course, your caller ID shows that it's Ben Affleck calling. Girl, that may be a once-in-a-lifetime opportunity worth losing your job over!)

◆**Fully charge your cell phone or PDA.** Don't miss your first real estate client meet-n-greet because your Palm Pilot ran out of juice.

◆**Identify yourself at the top of the conversation** during a "cold call." No, a "cold call" has nothing to do with your body temperature. A "cold call" is when you've never been introduced to nor have a relationship with the receiver. Give your name and the name of the company on whose behalf you're calling. If you're inquiring about an open position, say so up front.

◆**Learn as much about the person you're calling as possible** to identify an immediate commonality with someone you barely know. Simple similarities, such as your having attended the same college, were in the same sorority, grew up in the same region of the country or know someone in common make for the best ice-breakers. Avoid freaking her out by purging every detail you learned about her from the Internet — like her home address, date of birth or what she's looking for in a mate according to her personal online dating survey. But, at the very least, know how to properly enunciate her name.

◆ **Speak with a positive and healthy attitude.** People like happy people. It often puts them in a good mood too.

DON'T . . .

◆ **Assume all information is received in a timely fashion.** Sometimes text messages and voicemails don't appear promptly (or at all), especially if you or the receiver is in a bad signal area.

Hip Tip *Faxes don't always transmit properly. Always follow up with a phone call within a reasonable timeframe if you don't receive a prompt reply.*

◆ **Don't disrespect the caller by multi-tasking** during your phone conversation. Emailing or instructing your assistant on a project while taking a call with a colleague shows your lack of attention to the caller's needs. Trust us, even if you think you're being discreet, your non-verbal cues speak louder than you think.

◆ **Don't be annoying with your persistence.** Be clear, we're not saying don't be persistent. But know the boundaries. Don't pull a scene from the movie *Swingers!* Showing desperation and frustration through your phone manners isn't going to work in the work world. Today's modern technology makes anonymity almost obsolete. Do leave a brief message once with your name, number and a Cliff Note about why you're calling. If you haven't heard back in a week (unless you're calling about something that's more pressing), call again. This time, don't leave a message. If possible, just ask the assistant for a good time to call back. If after a couple more tries you can't get your foot in the door, consider leaving another message for him or her to call you back. And if you still don't get a return call, consider pursuing someone else to achieve your goal. This cat-and-mouse game just might be out of your control and not worth wasting your time on (just like the guy you've been chasing at the coffee shop who's got your digits but never calls).

Hip Tip *When making a cold call to a client or potential employer, befriend the assistant. This is the person who can help get your call returned quicker or redirect your call to someone who's better equipped to answer your questions. Ask his name, and if he doesn't seem rushed, develop a rapport with him. When you have to call again, remember to address him by name and identify yourself by the commonality you discovered. Assistants like feeling like they're important, too.*

◆ **Don't conduct important, private business calls** at a busy coffee shop or bookstore. You never know who's eavesdropping on your conversation and what they might do with their newfound information. And the person on the other end of the line might find it difficult to hear you with all that background noise. Be considerate of your latte neighbor, who's, perhaps, trying to have a morning coffee or read the newspaper in solitude.

◆ **Don't automatically put someone on speakerphone.** Ask your client if it's okay first. Be sure to say why: Whether you have someone else in the room who wants to sit in on the call or you just want to free your hands to look up important information that arises during your phone meeting.

Hip Tip *Pause every so often when presenting via teleconferencing. Ask if the other end has any questions or comments. There's nothing worse than being on the other end of the call and having your important question or comment go unheard because the presenter and participants are filling up the sound waves with unnecessary and inconsiderate chatter.*

◆ **Don't start a conversation or leave a message that begins with,** "I'm not sure if you're the right person or not, but . . ." Honey, let us tell you, if you give the receiver an easy out, he'll take it. (Hip Girls like the confidence of a man who tells us what day and time he's taking us out. Confidence in business matters is equally cherished.) Just tell him up front why you're calling. If he's not the right person, let him be the judge. Then ask him for contact information for the person who is more appropriate to handle your inquiry.

◆ **Don't call when it's just convenient to you.** Call when it's convenient to the recipient. If you're calling internationally or cross-country to swap stock market information, consider the time difference and the urgency of the matter first. Respect deadlines. Does he file his story in the afternoon or do his classes let out midday? Call at a time when reaching the other person is likely and when talking won't be highly disruptive to his schedule.

Video Killed the Telephone Star

You may knock 'em dead with your charm on the phone, but welcome to the era of dirt-cheap videoconference calls. Now what'cha gonna do? Woo everyone with your non-verbal skills, too, of course!

◆ **Look alive.** Slouching or twirling in your chair, cupping your head in your hands or kicking your feet up on the chair beside you are all signs of someone who'd rather be out surfing or shopping. Even in the most casual work environments, looking invested and enthusiastic about the company's success is half the battle in keeping and succeeding in your job.

Hip Tip *Even if you're zoned out from boredom, be alert enough to your surroundings to feign interest. Offer brief, positive, non-verbal and verbal reinforcement whenever it makes sense. Chuckle when the boss does, flip the* *pages of the document when everyone else does and offer a "hmmmm" or nod that reflects your understanding of the matter. And, for goodness sake, don't ask a question or make a comment if you haven't been paying attention. Nonverbal reinforcement, in this case, will be your best friend.*

◆ **Wait for your colleague** on the West Coast to complete her thought before beginning yours. Videoconferencing usually comes with a few seconds' delay. Don't pull a Janet Jackson. Use the delay to edit your response and allow your colleague to complete hers.

◆ **Sit in a prominent position** where the people who can make or break your career can clearly see you. Don't hide off to the side. This is your opportunity to be seen and heard by the president of the company who rarely sees you due to the coastal divide, or because your assistant-level responsibilities rarely put you in the spotlight.

◆ **Just because they can't see it on the screen** doesn't mean they can't interpret misbehaving. You may think you're being discreet about making funny faces or emailing someone on your PDA under the table as your boss at the other end of the camera makes her boring presentation. Think again. Even if you hide it behind reading material, an observant participant might figure out that something obnoxious is happening behind the paper.

◆ **Talk to both ends of the camera.** Address both the people in the room with you and those peering through the lens. If you'll be presenting, sit near the end of the table that faces the group in the room with you. This will allow you to address both audiences near and far more easily.

◆ **The meeting may have officially ended,** but don't talk smack in front of the videoconference equipment. Everyone on the other end may be out of the camera's view but still in the room, or you may think you were disconnected properly when you weren't. If you can't stop yourself from making fun of the new girl's hairdo, wait until you completely exit the videoconference room to do it.

◆ **Dress to impress the most important person** in the meeting, even if it's your fashion editor videoconference-calling all the way from Paris. Besides the fact that the Juicy Couture jumpsuit fad is fading, it doesn't exactly scream, "I want to be here." Your enthusiasm for your work is communicated through your attire, even millions of miles away.

Hip Tip *Avoid accessories that hide or detract from your face. Hats or overbearing headscarves make focusing on what you're saying even more difficult from far away. Wear clothes that lend credibility to your authority and your business, not attire that suggests you belong in the circus.*

◆ **Know how to use technology properly** before incorporating it into your presentation. PowerPoint and video quickly lose their luster, especially for the people millions of miles away, when you spend the first 15 minutes of your presentation trying to get the technology to work. If possible, have an audio/video specialist at your disposal to operate the equipment.

◆ **Fax, email or snail mail handouts and prototypes** to your East Coast participants before the meeting. Engaging participants' interest from a distance is challenging. Make sure they feel connected by distributing to them all the materials that your local employees will be receiving.

Hip Tip *Whether you're presenting via videoconference or regular ol'-fashioned in person, we suggest you hone your presentation style to be the most effective speaker possible. For more guidance on leading a meeting, we suggest* *you check out the book* KNOCKOUT PRESENTATIONS: HOW TO DELIVER YOUR MESSAGE WITH POWER, PUNCH, AND PIZZAZZ *by Diane Diresta. It gives more in-depth information on how to be a star presenter.*

Email: Mr. Postman of the New Frontier

Emailing with Style

Okay, now that you know the major functions at your fingertips for building and maintaining relationships in the modern world, it's equally important to know how to finesse the content of the email. (Think of how you learned to "work" your mom and dad whenever you missed your curfew in high school.) One inadvertent or misunderstood statement could ignite an office "fire" within seconds. So instead of playing firefighter, be proactive with these email safety measures.

◆ **Practice anger management.** Control your impulses to write an email while you're angry. Construct it and then sit on it for a day (if possible). Were you respectful? Did you edit it to take out the emotional attack? Are you CC-ing strictly the people who need to know what's up? (CC-ing is the term for copying other people on an email that's addressed to the attention of another recipient.) Talk facts and logic and leave the feelings for your personal relationships. Come back to the email. Re-read it before sending it to the masses.

□ **Bad example:** "I asked for your status reports by end of day today, and yet have only received one report thus far. Please send me your reports ASAP!"

□ **Good example:** "I am compiling the status reports that were due at the end of today. If you have not yet sent yours, can you please do so right away? Thank you."

◆ **Write a request — not a demand** — when you need help from people who don't necessarily need you. Perhaps you've taken charge of gathering all the information for your graduate group's report on the future of cloning. Don't let your Type A personality (hey, it's okay to own it) get the best of you. Remember, just because you care about getting an "A" on the report doesn't mean everyone in your group does. Learn from the contestant's mistakes on the TV series *The Apprentice* — use encouragement to motivate the people who can help you get the job done. Otherwise, they could spitefully make it more difficult. Construct your email to request help, not demand it. Using "please" and "thank you" doesn't automatically make your request inviting.

Check it out:

☐ **Bad example:** "Since I'm compiling our information for the thesis due on Monday, please send me your report by Friday. Thank you."

☐ **Good example:** "I'll happily volunteer to compile our findings for our group thesis. Could you please send your individual report to me by Friday so I can type it up over the weekend? Let me know if that doesn't work for you."

◆ **Use humor and irony sparingly.** Nothing is more easily misconstrued in emails than sarcasm because you don't get vocal inflections or facial expressions to back it up.

◆ **Save your fancy formatting for attached documents.** The body of an email is best left to simplicity. Otherwise, replying might become more difficult, especially if the format becomes distorted during transmission.

◆ **Brevity is a beautiful thing.** Keep your emails short, sweet and to the point. Hip Girls are inundated with information overload and don't have time to read a diary. Write, read and edit whatever is unnecessary.

◆ **Don't send emails you don't want others to see** (like your plans for ditching the company). Forwarding information is way too easy. Plus, your company's computer support team usually has access to your company email and can monitor what you're sending when you least expect it.

◆ **Watch your accessory style.** No, we aren't talking couture, ladies. We mean the way you fashion your email with extra "accessories" like bolding, "flagging" as urgent, italicizing, font style and size, punctuation choice, underlining, and computer symbols and acronyms like face-making :0) or LOL. Just like in fashion, over-accessorizing deflects attention from the areas you want to stand out. The same is true when constructing an email. For example: DON'T USE ALL CAPS. Nothing SCREAMS at someone more. Also, using exclamation marks can really make a statement! So only use them when appropriate! Get the picture?!!!!!

◆ **Is the content of the email better spoken?** If it'll end up taking you more time to correct a misunderstood email than it would to just pick up the phone and talk the message through, then call. It'll save you and everybody else who ends up CC'd on the email a whole lot of unnecessary political headaches.

◆ **Use email for rapid exchange of positive messaging.** It's a great way to commend, encourage or apologize to someone publicly.

◆ **Loop everyone in on a project.** Email is great for keeping track of the marketing proposal's approval status. You've got a paper trail to document everyone's comments.

◆ **Keep attachments to a minimum.** You don't want to cram up your clients' computers. Also, try to send them in a form easy for the recipient to open.

Hip Tip *Keep business emails separate from your personal ones. Consider opening a second account strictly for personal use. Some providers, such as Hotmail at hotmail.com, offer basic email accounts for no charge at all!*

◆ **Take extra precautions when sending mass emails.** Make sure to BCC (blind carbon copy), which allows the sender to hide a recipient's address from the rest of the recipients whose email addresses you can see.) And, really, is it necessary to hit "Reply All" if you just have a side note about the author's choice of wording? Here's a chance to take the high road and salvage her dignity by replying strictly to her.

◆ **Make your subject line text clear and concise.** This helps the receiver prioritize your email accordingly.

◆ **Proof-text your message before sending it.** Make sure your spell check and grammar devices are activated on your email service. It's a quick and easy way to check your spelling and protect your credibility.

◆ **Know your company's email policies.** Do you need HR approval to send out company-wide emails alerting people to your departure from the company? What's their take on sending or receiving personal emails through your work email address? Is old email purged periodically and, if so, how often? Or can your old mail be read a couple years back when you were calling your boss all kinds of names in emails to your friends during your battle for a raise? And how about the policy on sending and receiving sexually explicit material through email? Imagine explaining that one to your next potential employer when you're asked why you got fired. Bottom line here, ladies, is know what your company's limitations are and don't email anything you're not comfortable with your boss reading. You decide for yourselves what boundaries you feel comfortable pushing.

—⊶⊷—

Hip Girls were born with the gift to communicate. But just like our fashion sense, it requires honing our gift of gab to reach professional success.

Colleague Camaraderie:
Building (Not Burning) Bridges

———— ⦿⦿⦿ ————

"Slaving away at several PR and journalism internships paid off big after I finally got my undergraduate degree. I scored my first job with the paper I'd done my last internship for and with the boss who had mentored me. Great, right? Yeah, except that one co-worker was threatened that I was some seven years her junior and that she was competing with me, the former intern, for bylines. Despite our coastal divide, a tenuous work relationship ensued. No matter how diplomatic I tried to be, she never accepted or respected me or my work. Luckily, after a year of sticking it out and walking on eggshells whenever I had to deal with her, our bosses decided to can her! Okay, I admit it, I was ecstatic!"

— Denise, 23, Print Journalist

Your workplace can be a great way to meet people like you, with similar backgrounds, interests or goals. But just like there were plenty of people in school who couldn't have been more different than you (like the clique of girlie girls who worried all day about their perfect make-up), you're going to encounter some individuals in your business with distinctly different personalities than you would typically align yourself with. Not getting along with a co-worker can be a drag, or worse, being ousted by the office "clique" can sting. (Remember how it felt to be chosen last for a game of dodge ball when you were in elementary school? Ouch!) As important as it is to be productive and successful with the task at hand, your ability to play nice with the other "kids in the class" is often a determining factor for your ability to move ahead in your career.

Identify Your and Your Colleagues' Social Styles

Utilize your individual strengths in your job to show your boss and teammates just what you're made of (see the "Working Your Assets" chapter). But just like in the television show "Survivor," no matter how good you are at what you do, there are few jobs where you need only to rely on yourself. Keeping that in mind, building alliances with people you work with — even the colleagues you secretly loathe — is critical for survival and success at your place of employment. Therefore, understanding how to effectively meet the communication needs of a "talker" teammate, a "kiss-up" colleague or a "bully" or a "busy-body" co-worker will only help you achieve your goal.

We created a quiz (under the Social Identifier section) based on TRACOM Group's Social Style Model™ to help you determine which of the four social styles that all people fall under most represents you and your co-workers' styles. Note that no style is right or wrong or better than another. They are simply different (like your taste in fashion from your mother's). And just like in friendships, differences can make for exciting adventures. A word to the wise: This is simply to be used as a general guide. Deal with each situation and individual independently. Like a pair of jeans, these suggestions are not one-size-fits-all. With that in mind, apply the seven principles below as you attempt to identify a person's social style.

◆ **Don't be too quick to define a style.** Blanketing one particular move or statement into an overall behavior could inaccurately categorize a person's style. Some behaviors or actions are situational. (After all, you wouldn't want a new teammate to presume you're not the "sharpest tool in the shed" simply because you made one silly mistake.) It is consistent and repeated behavioral patterns that you should take note of.

◆ **Get out of the way.** In business, don't let your feelings interfere. Concentrate on how the other person is acting and what works with that person to get what you need.

◆ **Learn to observe accurately** and describe what a person does without making premature "good," "bad," or "why" judgments.

◆ **Separate style clues from workplace roles,** like positions of authority or subordinates. For instance, just because you're an assistant doesn't mean being in charge isn't important to you.

◆ **Most people have a dominant behavior style** that will drive their actions.

◆ **Unusual situations, previous experiences and new roles** might be the impetus for a behavior not typical of someone's dominant style habits.

◆ **Your perception of your own style** might be different from how others perceive you.

The Social Style Identifier Quiz*

Okay, ladies. You're throwing a bridal shower for a work friend. Answer each of the questions below. Select the response that best fits what you'd do in each situation. At the end, tally the number of a, b, c and d answers. Whichever you have the most of is likely to be your dominant Social Style. Then, for fun, have a friend take the quiz, based on how she thinks you'd behave in each situation. But don't influence her decisions. That won't give you an accurate reflection of how others perceive your Social Style.

1. **First up: Where, when and what time is the party?**
   a. You carefully choose a handful of dates and times and thoroughly research all your venue options. You can't decide, so you ask your colleagues for their opinions. After weighing their thoughts, you decide you'll do a walk-through of each of the places you've come up with before making any of the where, when and time logistical decisions.
   b. You brainstorm a few venue possibilities and call them to check that they meet each of your day, time and budget needs. You inquire with the bride-to-be if she has a preference. She doesn't, so you choose a venue and go for it.

---

* This quiz is intended to help you understand what your Social Style might be. It uses the concepts of TRACOM's Social Style Model, but was not provided by TRACOM, which designs and uses empirically verified assessment instruments.

Adapted for use and used by permission of The TRACOM Group. For more information about Social Style visit: The TRACOM Group at www.tracomcorp.com, or call 1-800-221-2321.

c. You poll the bride-to-be and colleagues for their availability and ideas for venues. After pairing them with your own suggestions and investigating that they meet your criteria, you select places you're most familiar with.

d. You consult the bride-to-be and pick a date, time and place. You get so caught up in creating the party's theme and games that you almost forget to send out your "save the date" invitations. Thank God for Evite!

2. A couple of your colleagues volunteer to help you throw the party. You:

a. Thank them and create a list of items you need accomplished, then ask each of the volunteers which of the tasks they'd like to tackle.

b. Tell them you appreciate their offer, and that if you find that you need help, you'll definitely ask them.

c. Thank them and ask them to come along to the venue. You'd like their opinion on how to decorate. Then, together, you shop 'til you drop for the decorations.

d. Thank them again, and then lunge into your fabulous "wine-tasting" theme, complete with all but a ribbon-cutting ceremony. For their part, you tell them it'd be great if they'd pick up various kinds of wine for the actual wine-tasting portion of the party.

3. It's the morning of the party. You get to the cake shop and discover they've made a few mistakes on your decoration instructions. You:

a. Run to your car where you have your handy dandy bridal shower notebook. In it, you have filed away your receipt with exact instructions for your cake selection, which proves you are right. You have plenty of time for them to change it, but you waiver on whether you should just take the "wrong" cake and take them up on their offer for a marginal refund or pay the full price and get exactly what you asked for.

b. Simply don't have time to wait for them to re-do the cake. You decide on their discount offer since it was their mistake.

c. Call the girls who have been helping you out and enlist their opinions about your predicament.

d. Cover your face with both your hands; you can't believe this is happening! But then you have a light bulb moment: If they'd just add some frosting here and some fresh roses there, it'd look just as beautiful, if not more so, than what you'd originally envisioned. (And yes, you'll tell them you'd still like a discount, please.)

4. **You arrive at the venue:**

a. An hour early to measure the room with the most attention to detail. You want to ensure that your decorating idea will be executed flawlessly.

b. As you'd planned. You jump into overdrive and start tackling the duties you've already assigned. But as soon as help arrives, you quickly delegate decorating, cooking and guest-book responsibilities almost in military-like fashion.

c. And greet everyone as they show up. With a few early birds, you deliberate and delegate your orders and needs for the games, cake and gift-opening.

d. About 30 minutes later than you'd hoped. You're feeling a bit harried because you have a few last-minute details to delegate. But once it's all finished, you're quite sure everyone will agree, this party's going to be the best bridal shower they've ever attended.

5. **It was a marvelous party and it's time to wrap things up. You:**
    a. Thank everyone for coming and systematically begin clean up.
    b. Thank everyone for coming and inform them that for anyone who might be up for it, the next-door pub has everyone's names on the guest list for a nightcap.
    c. Revel with some lingering partygoers about what a lovely time was had as you share in clean-up duties. Then join the bride-to-be and rest of the gang who have already got the party in full swing elsewhere.
    d. Announce to everyone that you've decided to make your party an annual event. And just as everyone applauds your proclamation, you holler, "I'm not ready for the party to end. Why don't you all come over to my pad tonight for a night cap?"

Tally your answers. Refer to the descriptions to extrapolate your most dominant responses and their meanings.

MOSTLY "A'S"

◆ **Analytical style.** The Analytical Style is thinking oriented, statistical, distant and logical. Cool, independent, yet cooperative. They're disciplined about time and somewhat slow to act. People of the Analytical Style rely on facts and avoid risks. Their approach to relationships is to ask questions and control their emotions. They project an image of good planners, organizers and problem-solvers with the ability to work out tasks systematically. Because of their apparent concern for facts and logical, serious organization of thought, coupled with a desire to be "right," the Analytical person often displays a reluctance to declare or commit to a position.

Mostly "B's"

◆ **Driving style.** The Driving Style person is action oriented, independent, cool and has a "do it my way" approach. As a result, he appears to know what he wants and becomes impatient with delays. He's competitive and tends to focus primarily on the immediate timeframe. Because of his focus on results and goals, he seems to show little concern for the feelings of others or for personal relationships. Some consider his actions harsh, severe or critical since he gives such limited attention to relationships. Others may consider this behavior efficient and decisive. The Driving Style seeks control through the use of power in situations that might deny him the freedom to act as he wishes to achieve his objectives.

Mostly "C's"

◆ **Amiable style.** The Amiable Style person is relationship-oriented, supportive, likeable and a team player. He's warm, approachable and cooperative. Amiable persons frequently stick with the comfortable and known, appearing slow or reluctant to change. They promote teamwork and collaboration by eliciting the feelings and thoughts of others affected by the topic at hand. The Amiable person's concern for others often lends joy, warmth and freshness to situations.

Mostly "D's"

◆ **Expressive style.** The Expressive Style person is intuition-oriented, personable and impulsive. He's approachable and warm, yet competitive for recognition. He acts quickly, with many decisions based on opinions. The Expressive Style is based on giving opinions and displaying emotions. As a result, some see the Expressive person's behavior as flighty, changeable, impractical, emotional and opinionated. He tends to appear more imaginative and creative with his ideas than other styles. Expressive people can generate enthusiasm in others, and their behavior can be intensely stimulating, exciting and fun for others who get caught up in the person's behavior.

Hip Tip *For more information on all the interpersonal communication skills and resources that the* TRACOM *Group has to offer, contact them by phone at (800) 221-2321, or visit their Website at www.tracomcorp.com.*

Become a Chameleon

Perhaps even more important than determining your own behavior is determining your ability to meet others' style needs. If you can't beat them, join them, or so the saying goes. Adapting just enough to a coworker's work style to achieve your goal is a true asset in and of itself. So win your colleagues over. Learn the art of compromise. It's a skill you can use at work and at home. And we're not suggesting that you always give in to others. Goodness, gracious, no! Hip Girls wouldn't date a guy without a backbone, so we certainly wouldn't advocate that you lose your own in personal or office relationships either. We're talking about doing something for others and finding a middle ground for fair play. And recognize that sometimes being a Hip Girl requires you to extend your hand first to help a colleague reach out. The TRACOM Group experts suggest how.

Succeed with an analytical style
  Do . . .
  ☐ Prepare your case in advance, providing accurate and realistic information, based on solid, tangible and practical evidence.

- ☐ Stick to business. (Don't digress onto your plans for the weekend ski trip with your old sorority clan when you're in the middle of nailing down details for the big client meet-n-greet.)
- ☐ Support their principles, but list pros and cons to make suggestions.
- ☐ Take your time, but be persistent.
- ☐ Give them time to verify the reliability of your actions.
- ☐ Minimize the risk involved.

DISLIKES . . .
- ☐ Disorganization or messiness.
- ☐ A giddy, casual, informal or loud approach.
- ☐ Ambiguities about expectations or results.
- ☐ Personal incentives or communication, including threats, cajoling, whimpering or coaxing.
- ☐ Using opinions as evidence. (Don't postulate that about two-thirds of women prefer their men in boxers over briefs when, in fact, you can't support your claim with evidence.)
- ☐ Pushiness and unrealistic deadlines

Succeed with an amiable style

Do . . .
- ☐ Break the ice with a personal comment. (Compliment them, inquire about their family, or, if they've been under the weather, how they're feeling.)
- ☐ Show interest in them as people. Be candid and honest.
- ☐ Inquire about their personal goals by listening and being responsive to them.
- ☐ Ask "how" questions to draw their opinions.

□ If you disagree with them, look for hurt feelings, personal reasons.
□ Move casually and informally.
□ Define individual contributions.
□ Provide guarantees that their decision will minimize risks.
□ Offer personal assurances.

DISLIKES . . .
□ Don't attack.
□ Don't rush into an agenda.
□ Avoid sticking coldly to business.
□ Don't coerce them into making quick responses by limiting their options with statements like, "Here's how I see it."
□ Avoid a domineering or dominating approach.
□ Don't debate facts and figures.
□ Don't manipulate, patronize or demean them into agreeing.
□ Avoid abrupt and rapid movements.
□ Avoid ambiguities; limit options and probabilities.
□ Don't keep deciding for them, or they'll lose initiative. Give them a chance to speak. (Just because they may not be the first to offer up their opinion doesn't mean they don't have one.)

Succeed with an expressive style
Do . . .
□ Plan interactions that support their dreams and intentions.
□ Leave time for relating and socializing.
□ Talk about people and their goals.
□ Ask their opinions, ideas and hunches and then offer yours. (Feed their egos about their ideas and opinions, and, girl, you're half-way to getting what your heart desires.)

□ Provide ideas for implementing action.

□ Use your time in a stimulating, fun-loving and fast-moving manner.

□ Provide testimonials from people they see as important and prominent.

□ Offer special, immediate and extra incentives for their willingness to take risks.

□ Allow time for discussing ideas.

DISLIKES . . .

□ Avoid a curt, cold or tight-lipped approach.

□ Avoid a deluge of facts, figures, alternatives and abstractions.

□ Don't waste time trying to be impersonal and judgmental.

□ Don't "dream" with them, or you'll lose.

□ Don't talk down to them.

□ Don't be dogmatic.

Succeed with a driving style

Do . . .

□ Be clear, specific, brief and to the point.

□ Present the facts logically, and plan your presentation efficiently.

□ Ask specific "what" questions.

□ Provide alternatives and choices for them to make their own decisions.

□ Offer facts and figures about the probability of success or effectiveness of options.

□ If you agree, support the facts, not the person. (For instance, "I see your point, and I think it's brilliant," not, "I'm with you.")

□ Motivate and persuade by referring to objectives and results.

□ After completing business, depart graciously.

DISLIKES . . .

- If you disagree with someone with a Driving Style, take issue with facts, not the person. (Avoid saying, "I don't think you're right," or "That's hardly accurate." You might as well have just screamed, "You're crazy" at him.) Simply ask a Driving Style person to explain, substantiate or illustrate her point; that way you don't appear to be attacking or disrespecting her opinions.
- Don't waste time, especially with personal talk, rhetorical or useless questions.
- Disorganization and forgetfulness drives them batty.
- Loopholes or cloudy issues leave Driving Style people unsettled.
- Do not tell a Driving Style person what to do.
- Wild speculation or questionable guarantees and assurances do not set well with them.
- Whether you agree or disagree, don't make it a personal point.
- Avoid convincing through "personal" means.
- People who ramble on after business is done drive them crazy. Close shop and get out.

Hip Tip *You might perceive that behavior at home is different in your personal life. The TRACOM Group's experts say that although you may demonstrate the typical behaviors of various styles, you're unlikely to change your dominant style behaviors. Your ability to "switch gears" is more of a reflection of your ability to be versatile.*

Now that you're on your way to better communication with your colleagues, you may be faced with whether or not to develop a more intimate relationship with them. No, we're not talking about an office romance (although if you're considering that, better check out our "Foreplay for Fair Play" chapter). Rather, we're talking about building rapport beyond doing business through after-work drinks, company-sponsored family barbecues or joining the office softball team. So be sure to read the following:

The Hip Girl's Top 10 for Making Work-Friends

1. **Friends don't let friends talk drunk** at work functions. At the first sign that your alcohol-induced motor-mouth might be kicking into overdrive, ask a work-friend to take you home or cab it.

Hip Tip *If you live near some of your co-workers, see if they'd be interested in carpooling a few times a week. It'll help save you both some cash, while sparking up your normally dull morning commute. It's also a perfect chance to get to know somebody. Plus, no one said you can't stop for happy hour after a long, hard day.*

2. **Play with the boys,** but don't be a boy. The guys may be doing keg-stands and strip-dancing on top of the bar, but a Hip Girl doesn't take it that far. While guys like a guy's-girl — a chick who watches sports, tells jokes or tosses back an occasional beer — guys don't want to see their "li'l sis" completely lose her feminine touch. Skip the belching and farting contest and take a pass on the dare to bare your assets. Trust us, they won't respect you for it in the morning, no matter how much they may try to convince you otherwise in the late hours of the evening.

3. **Tread slowly in building your friendship** outside of the office. Establish boundaries and space from the get-go. Just like in love,

it's hard to turn back the clock. Pulling back on the reigns of your friendship after you've been tied to the hip — especially if it's one-sided — may be very upsetting to your work-friend.

Hip Tip Enjoy hiking? How about yoga? Chances are if you do, someone at your work does too. Invite a coworker to join you for an afternoon hike or a cleansing lunchtime yoga class. Find a common pastime, outside of the office, to help a burgeoning friendship.

4. **Avoid office gossip.** Work might be the one thing you have in common, but use your time at out-of-office functions with colleagues or your bosses to find another commonality and interest. This will help make your work-designated conversations flow more smoothly because of the vested personal attachment outside of the office.

5. **Be a good listener to a colleague** who wants to dish on work or talk shop, but try to avoid explicitly commenting or advising on the matter while you're playing golf. (We know, the temptation to commiserate is tough. And the truth is, there will be times you will likely get caught up in it. Just check yourself and resist temptation the next time.) After indulging her need to vent and acknowledging that you've heard her, attempt to discreetly transition into another non-work-related conversation. If the out-of-office venting becomes consistent and wearing, consider a more blunt but polite approach: "You know, we work such long and hard hours that our personal time is really precious. Let's just focus on having fun together unless we're on company hours."

6. **Give up some details about your personal life,** but be wary of discussing something you'd never want someone else in your office to

know about — like your one-night make-out session with the hot-tie in the cubicle next to yours or your secret mission to jockey for a promotion. Even though you may shop 'til you drop together, you're still healthy competitors at the office. Strike a balance about what you divulge (because not divulging any information about your life can just as easily work against you). If you feel the urge to splurge on personal details to your work friend, save your deepest, darkest secrets until after you've jumped ship for a new company where you no longer pose a threat to her career advancement.

Hip Tip   *Generally speaking, some of the riskier conversational pieces to avoid with work friends are your personal experiences or opinions about politics, religion or sex-related topics.*

7. **Be selective** about which friends from your "inner circle" you introduce to your work friend. If they don't get along, you don't want that on your hands. Also, before fusing groups of friends, you'd better make it clear to your personal friends to keep their mouths shut about the pet names you've given your work mates — like Snaggle-Tooth or the Boss's Little Mini-me — or other pertinent personal information you don't want your work-friend to pick up.

8. **Consider the appropriateness of activities** you undertake before inviting your work friend to tag along. Only you can judge what will work depending on the confines of your relationship.

9. **Don't blatantly alienate co-workers** from out-of-office excursions. Be discreet about only inviting a few co-workers to your baby shower. Consider a systematic selection (like extending an invitation to your immediate teammates only) so that the others can't take the rejection personally.

If you're clearly on the outskirts of the company clique, occasionally initiate your own integration by inviting one or two of the "inner" work circle members to lunch. Targeting a couple of people to champion your acceptance gives you a better chance at fitting in with the clique. But don't be overzealous with your attempt, or your colleagues will view you as clingy and desperate. And no one likes someone who tries too hard. Just be yourself so people can appreciate you for who you really are, not someone you want them to see.

10. **If you decide you need to disengage** from your work friendship, do it slowly and discreetly. Don't talk smack about your friend to your other work-friends. And don't withdraw your friendship overnight. Start by decreasing your availability to hang out or chat on the phone. Disengaging your friendship over a short time will make it look like your lives are growing in separate directions, instead of making it appear like a personal attack on her character.

At the end of the workday, we're all human, and even the coldest of co-workers want to feel liked, included or, at the very least, respected.

Boss Behavior:

Dazzling and Dealing with the Person Who Signs Your Paycheck

"I had asked for a promotion and was really hurt and angry when my boss filled the position with someone from outside of the company. And while I genuinely liked my boss, her decision created a rift in our relationship. After taking some time off, I decided that if I wanted to get ahead in the department, I needed to make our relationship work. When I returned, I made a conscience effort to exercise more patience and to flex more to her work-style. About four months later, I got the promotion, and, ever since, my boss has been my biggest cheerleader. In retrospect, I am grateful she insisted I learn how to be more versatile and compassionate toward others' needs, while getting my needs met too."

— Jennifer, 31, Director in Entertainment PR
and Author

A boss can make or break your job. Whether your work leaves you uninspired or you've landed your dream job, selecting a boss you get along with is significant to both your daily happiness and career success. So whether you're simply interviewing for a position or you find yourself immersed in corporate culture, read the following pointers on managing your relationship with the person who can adversely affect your happiness.

Court Your Boss

Whether you've been at your job for three years or you've barely settled your pooch's picture next to your computer, invest a little time getting to know your boss. Get a feel for where she is in her life, from her work to personal hobbies. This will help you know a good time to hit her up for a pay increase (see "Nailing the Negotiations" chapter), how to tell her about your mistake or how receptive she might be to new ideas in the workplace. (Think of it like dating or marriage. Knowing just how and when to ebb and flow with your sweetie makes attending your family's vacation or your shopping excursions more bearable for him . . . and, ultimately, for you.) Size up your boss in advance regarding how she handles and receives information. Take time to authentically ingratiate her with the utmost integrity. Courting your boss will enlighten you on how to approach her about various situations. This will lay the foundation for a strong work relationship and will give you an edge for getting the most out of your position.

◆ **Greet your boss each day,** but make sure she's had a few moments to settle in. Nothing fancy, no long, drawn-out conversations are required. A simple smile and "Good morning" or "How was your evening?" will suffice. Each day might require a little more or little less interaction, depending on how harried she appears, or how ingrained she is in returning phone calls, emails, or preparing for an early morning meeting.

◆ **Inquire about her personal life.** Some bosses aren't at all interested in mixing business with pleasure. But showing genuine interest in the well-being of your boss, colleagues and clients is generally a great way to build a strong relationship beyond "Yes ma'am," "No ma'am." Only you can gauge how comfortable your boss is in sharing personal information. Start out with generic personal questions like, "Did you have a nice weekend? What did you do?" or "How's your family?" If she squirms or balks at such inquiries, then you certainly don't want to dive into a subject more personal.

◆ **Share select information about your personal life with your boss.** Strike a balance by sharing generic pieces of your daily life (like your kids are in Kung Fu classes or you've been dating someone for several months, or you saw a great movie that you think she might like), while keeping the more intimate details to yourself (like you're considering a divorce, you're lonely or you're bored to tears with your job). Only you can establish safe boundaries with your relationship. Be clear, though. Even if you have a tight-knit bond with your boss, in the end, what is good for business must override personal strife. So if you decide to give up the goods about your break-up with your beau because you're almost certain your boss will be compassionate to your sensitive mood (which, by the way, we rarely suggest you do), reinforce that it will not affect your productivity. Perhaps approach it this way: "I just wanted to let you know if I'm not my typical cheerful self these next couple of weeks, it has nothing to do with work. In fact, I'm thrilled to be back to work because Mark and I broke up over New Year's. Throwing myself into my job is exactly what I need to keep my mind off of personal matters."

Hip Tip Do not tell your boss (or your colleagues and clients) your age. Nor should you blab about adventures in your life (like late-night rages) that will scream your age. Whether you're 24 or 34, this can work against you in most lines of business. If you are on the younger side, people may automatically project certain traits of immaturity, inexperience or irresponsibility onto you. (Exceptions may be if you're in a youth-obsessed career like acting or writing where being young assumes you're more in touch with your audience.) On the flip side, announcing your more mature age may conjure up negative associations such as you're over-qualified, inflexible for travel (especially if you have a family), will need time off due to health issues or you're not hip with your younger clients. Instead, let your experience, success and coiffed business etiquette speak on your behalf. If someone point blank asks your age, try darting the question with a generic answer, perhaps in a joking manner. Try, "I look younger than I am, trust me," "I'm old enough to know better than to tell you," "Don't you know it's rude to ask a lady her age," or "It's my worldly experience that keeps me young (or seem wise beyond my years)." Simply put: Keep 'em guessing.

◆ **Tune into your boss's communication needs.** Get face-to-face time (or ear-to-ear in a long-distance relationship) at least once each day. Check in with her about what you've got going on or to see if she needs help on a project she's slamming on. Depending on your role or the project you're spearheading, you may need to be more accessible to your boss. For instance, maybe you're working on a high-priority initiative like a class field trip or an important client's finances. You may need to bring her up to speed more often because it'll make her feel more comfortable that the work is being done to her satisfaction. It also keeps her from being blindsided by a superior or colleague who quizzes her about the status of your project. Remember, everyone reports to someone. Empower your boss to look good, too. Typically, it will reflect positively on you.

Hip Tip *If you work on opposite coasts from your boss or you work mainly from home, communication with your boss is especially key. Make yourself more "visible" when facing geographical challenges. Touch base with your boss periodically throughout the day — both through phone conversation and email. But because you can't physically see how busy she is, be sure not to inundate her with unnecessary and long-winded conversations.*

◆ **Listen to your boss vent.** We all need to vent sometimes about our work; it's practically a rite of passage in the workforce. Lest we not forget, no matter how you feel about your boss, she's just as human as you are. So if your supervisor needs to blow off steam, and it's not at your expense, lend her an ear. You should feel honored she feels secure enough with your relationship to let her tongue rip.

Hip Tip *Long hours, swapping work war stories and sharing close quarters can sometimes lead to romance. If you find yourself falling in love or lust with your superior, don't rush into anything. Read our "Foreplay to Fairplay" chapter. Also check out the section called Fishing off the Company Pier in the "Colleague Camaraderie" chapter.*

◆ **Manage up.** When dating someone new, there's often a subliminal push-pull about your availability to hang out with your single gal pals and your desire for becoming immersed in your new, exciting "coupledom." Just as you manage yourself and your guy's expectations for what is acceptable in your relationship, you also need to strategically manage your supervisor about your limitations at work. This can be everything from your availability to put in long hours, to travel or skipping lunches. You will also need to manage up about your workload. Keep your boss informed about your status on projects, substantiating your unavailability for taking on more responsibility or requesting additional manpower to take on more leadership tasks.

◆ **Read your boss's work style** and flex to it. (See more in the Boss Style section or the "Colleague Camaraderie" chapter.) You're a visionary and your boss gets caught up in details. Perhaps your style is to work independently and make decisions, while your boss likes discussing matters and coming to conclusions together. Or you're more casual in your approach while she's more corporate. Different styles can make an even stronger team (that's how Nick Lachey and Jessica Simpson keep it together for sure). But just as in love you have to make the differences work in your favor, and you have to work diligently to assure your differences jive. Identify your boss's preferred work style and do your best to support her style with yours. This doesn't mean relinquishing your style to become more like her. It simply means incorporating what's important to your boss into your approach for handling matters.

Wheeling and Dealing with the Boss

What's your boss's work style? Is she a Chatty Cathy who makes it challenging for you to complete your work? Does she micro-manage even the simplest things? Does she like you by her side as she tends to her chores? Or perhaps she's a workaholic who expects your life to come second to your work. Whatever your situation, strategizing and compromising will help you to win your boss's favor and hopefully succeed in your future.

Gal Pal

Have you ever had a good guy friend whom you considered dating, but worried about losing the solid friendship if you took it to that next level? Taking your office relationship and turning it personal can be just as scary, with even more at risk, including your livelihood. From house- or dog-sitting for your boss to weekend ski trips with her and her hubby, evolving your business relationship into an out-of-office friendship has its pros and cons. Ultimately, you and your boss have to decide what feels comfortable. Consider some of the factors below before you make your call.

◆ **Pros**

   □   She will likely be more compassionate toward your work productivity, particularly if you're faced with personal strife, because she cares about your overall well-being — both at home and on the job.

   □   You may gain a friend and mentor.

   □   She will likely have your back if someone at work has it in for you.

   □   She will likely want to see you succeed and will be professionally supportive.

◆ **Cons**

   □   You could have a disagreement that she can't quite get over which would adversely affect you at work or in your personal relationship.

   □   Because she knows a lot about your personal life, it makes it more difficult to call in for a self-induced sick day off.

   □   At some point, you may want to minimize her involvement in your personal business. If you don't slowly withdraw, it could cause some serious hurt feelings and tension.

   □   Blurring the lines sometimes makes people a little too comfortable with each other, making taking advantage of the other person a possible subconscious outcome. This could put you or her in a compromising position at work.

Dodging the Gal Pal Draft

If you decide you're uncomfortable exploring a closer relationship with your supervisor, below are some tips for enabling you to work around her need to bond with you.

◆ **Avoid sharing intimate details of your life.** Sharing details you think she may not be interested in or discussing generic topics like sports, music, movies, restaurants or recipes may keep her at bay for the time being.

◆ **Steer clear of emotional outreach.** Hugs, kisses or pats are serious signs of closeness. Thwart her opportunities by positioning yourself across from her desk.

◆ **Offer social invitations you know she's not available for,** or interested in. By now you've probably experienced being pursued by someone you weren't into. You dodged hurting his feelings by "inadvertently" missing his call, accidentally losing his number or having plans for the night he's asked you out for. Likewise, check your boss's schedule. Once in a great while, invite her to join you for lunch when she's booked a client walk-thru. Corral her to join you for surfing, conveniently forgetting she's deathly afraid of water. Be believable, but just as creative when skirting your boss's interest in taking your office relationship personal.

Micro-manager

Does your supervisor want to know your whereabouts every second? Perhaps she wants to be cc'd on every email you receive or send.

Working for a micro-manager can be really frustrating and leave you feeling inadequate, unappreciated and restricted. As long as you're honest with yourself and putting your best foot forward, the first step in empowering yourself when dealing with a micro-manager boss is recognizing that her controlling disposition is her issue, not yours. Then:

◆ **Overload your manager with information.** Give details of everything you're doing. Do it both in writing and verbally.

◆ **Empower your boss** by involving her in the decision-making process, but position yourself as a leader by limiting her options. Like when you shop with your mother who graciously offers to treat you to a birthday shopping spree, then learn that with the gift comes a small price tag: Finding clothes she approves of. You strategically take her into only two or three stores where you can practically guarantee you'll find something you can both agree on. And just as you should make your mother feel like her opinion is valued by soliciting her advice about what looks good on you, you should do the same when addressing your boss about which decision is the most beneficial.

◆ **Bite your tongue and smile** when your boss tries to take over. Be open-minded to her suggestions while contemplating if it's a battle worth fighting. If it isn't, reinforce her position by saying something like, "I hadn't thought of that. What a good idea." If you truly don't agree with her, gently steer her back to your way of thinking. Try, "You know, I thought of that but here's why I thought this might work better," or "How about if we blend the two ideas?"

◆ **Put your best foot forward.** Your consistent reinforcement of a job well done and of her as a leader just might be enough to keep her nose away from where it doesn't belong.

The Work Maniac

You enjoy your work and take pride in a job well done. But when it's time to play, you're the first in line. So what do you do if your boss hasn't learned to take full advantage of the more important things in life, like an extra hour of sleep in the morning with your sweetie, catching a wave on your surfboard, coffee time with the girls or simply reading?

◆ **Bring the world to her.** Strategically lay the travel and leisure section of the newspaper out in the open where she might be more apt to pick it up and read it. When she asks about your personal life, mention a few really cool hobbies you enjoy, like cycling or dancing. Use water cooler conversation — like popular TV shows and movies, celebrities, sports, politics or the weather — that lends itself to life outside the office.

◆ **Showcase your family and interests.** Don't create a shrine in your office of your pride and joys, but do keep them top of mind by prominently displaying a few photos of them around your cubicle. If you're a proud Trojan, frame your USC football photo and hang it where your boss can appreciate it.

◆ **Encourage her personal interests.** If you see an article in a magazine about a hobby she enjoys, bring it in for her to read. Perhaps she likes baking or yoga, so email her a link you stumbled upon that offers unique cooking classes or yoga retreats in Fiji. If baseball is her thing, treat her with tickets to a home game.

◆ **Ask for time off as far in advance as possible.** Whenever possible, pick dates that you know work well in your upcoming workload schedule. That way when you request time off, you can position it as if you're putting your company's needs first.

◆ **Take the time off.** Don't abuse the system, but if you've requested time off, don't consistently reschedule your time-off plans because something important comes up at work. This sets an unhealthy precedent for your boss to expect it. Also, if you've got 10 sick days a year, use a few (maybe one every three or four months) . . . whether you need them or not. This might encourage her to do the same for herself.

The Credit Stealer

No, we're not talking about your stolen identity — that's a chapter in the first installment of *The Hip Girl's Handbook* series. We're talking about your credit-stealer supervisor who takes your ideas and runs with them, without ever crediting you in front of others for your efforts. It's disheartening and downright dirty for any supervisor to notoriously steal your thunder and never turn the spotlight back on you. Sadly, it's an old trick of the trade that happens more than you might think. Swimming among a bunch of credit-stealing sharks is going to test your survival skills for sure.

◆ **Making your boss look good** is part of your job, so if on occasion she doesn't divulge that you secured the sponsors for the event or that it was your investigative work that discovered the misappropriation of funds, let it slide. Every now and then, it's more important to be the support that helps your boss shine.

◆ **Document and organize your efforts.** Email, memos or phone messages are your saving grace when proving your worth. Keep your papers of proof organized so that if you need them to support your assertion, you can find them quickly.

◆ **Subtly inquire about asserting your presence** with colleagues, clients and other superiors. List your contact information in case anyone has questions about the science class field trip to the wilderness you've planned. Ask your boss if you can attend the meeting with her as her support system, and suggest that she can defer to you if others ask questions about the proposal you researched for her. Offer to fly to

New York to handle the meeting (only if, of course, it would be appropriate) if she's finding it challenging to accommodate it in her schedule. If she says no, don't push the issue. Just occasionally assert yourself again when other such opportunities arise.

◆ **Consider consulting your HR representative.** Documenting the credit-stealing ways of your boss with the human resources department might keep you in good graces with the company without jeopardizing too much of your current situation. But keep in mind that the human resources department is funded by your company's dollar.

◆ **Recognize when all is a lost cause.** If you've tried all you can to triumph over an insecure, attention-seeking boss, and your attempts are proved unsuccessful, perhaps it's time to go somewhere where your superiors will cheer your skills, knowledge and talents.

The No-Time-to-Talk Manager

You need an answer, but getting your foot in the door to get an answer from your boss is more difficult than getting tickets to the Olympics.

◆ **Befriend her assistant.** Sometimes getting what you need, including valuable face time, is a lot easier if her assistant likes you or knows the value of your information.

◆ **Ask the boss's assistant** to help you find 15-30 minutes in her busy schedule to meet with you on some important business matters.

◆ **Pop your face in the boss's office** when it's time for the meeting. If you don't show your face, it's unlikely she'll come looking for you. If she's in the middle of an important phone call, deeply engrossed in an email or in a closed-door meeting, come back every 20 to 30 minutes to check on her status. If possible, let her see your face. Eye contact makes it harder to blow off the meeting.

◆ **Present your options to resolve a situation** as a list that allows her to quickly approve or disapprove of the choices.

◆ **Don't waste her time with details** unless she asks. Stick to what you need, thank her, and get out.

◆ Whenever possible, and if your work responsibilities call for it, **request a weekly or biweekly 20-minute low-down session** for the same time to get answers to pressing matters.

The Flake

Do your boss's wishy-washy ways drive you up a wall? Not only can she not make a decision, she blames everyone else when she gets stuck in a rut? Or does she forget what she's promised or requested, and knows only how to be reactive instead of proactive?

◆ **Keep your cool.** Don't let her overly anxious ways make you blow your lid.

◆ **Keep two feet in front of her.** If she has a history of mentioning projects in passing but not saying anything again for a week, start gathering information before she brings it up again.

◆ **When she does inquire about the project,** deluge her with all that you know. Show her you're on top of it. Make yourself an indispensable asset to her flaky work style.

◆ **Ask the questions** you need her to answer as early in the project as possible before you move forward on it.

◆ **Help her be proactive.**

  ☐ Document your deadline needs. Fudge your deadline a day or a week prior to the actual deadline. This is a proactive way of preventing your boss's reactive style from affecting the outcome of your work. Perhaps create a monthly calendar noting preferred deadlines for your projects, then review it with your boss.

◻ Send occasional reminders. Either in a one-on-one meeting or in an email, gently remind your supervisor that you need an answer soon. Try, "Have you had an opportunity to think about how you want to handle the marketing strategy?" or "I'm meeting with my professor on Tuesday to go over my internship. Is there anything I can do to help you get that letter written to him?"

◻ In a non-threatening manner, remind her of other upcoming events, holidays or major lines of business. She may need to start thinking about how she's going to delegate the workload. Try, "I noticed that the industrial trade show is coming up in March, and I just want to offer to spearhead that project if you have your hands full," or, "I was just looking at the calendar and noticed that my two-week vacation to Europe is coming up quickly. We still need to finalize these details for the big investors' meeting before I take off. When works in your schedule for us to go over that?"

◆ **Bring other trusted colleagues on board,** when appropriate, so that they can be eyewitnesses to any future misunderstandings regarding the delegation and status of work.

◆ **At the end of the day, you'll never change your boss's ingrained work style.** You can only hope to ebb and flow with hers, or if you're really lucky, like this Hip Girl, subliminally influence hers with your style. Help yourself succeed by learning to work with it instead of against it.

Speak Your Boss's Language

We didn't want to leave you hanging. We think the information about how to identify your boss's approach to work and life is really important. It will give you insight on how to persuade her to give you what you want. Don't mind the fancy terminology for each description. Consider it a free crash course in psychology.

◆ **Collaborative:** Work through problems and solutions with your boss, roommates, etc.

◆ **Logical:** Present facts, evidence and reasons.

◆ **Emotional:** Talk feelings like excitement, guilt or competitiveness, or use her belief system to get her to see it your way. (This is the least preferred style for business interaction. But if your boss operates under this style, learn to flex with it.)

◆ **Futuristic:** Be a pioneer. Champion a vision of endless, realistic possibilities.

◆ **Positional:** Who's your daddy? Whether you have seniority or are a VIP, a vice president, teacher or guardian, use your high status as a means to back your position.

◆ **Expert:** Rely on your credibility and opinion as an expert to gain support.

◆ **Consultative:** Learn your boss's needs and problems and customize your ideas so your boss can see how they benefit his position.

◆ **Social:** We know, you're thinking it's martini time! Well, we don't recommend you discuss the future with your boss over alcohol. But for those who require a more social approach to deal-making, consider a walk-n-talk while grabbing coffee, or "massage" a client for her business over a game of golf.

Tips to Turn Your Boss's Head

What are some of the most basic ways to impress your boss? Score with your boss by practicing the following tips for getting ahead:

□   Take initiative
□   Manage and prioritize work appropriately

- ☐ Maintain your composure and practice flexibility
- ☐ Act with integrity
- ☐ Communicate and listen
- ☐ Build solid relationships
- ☐ Develop creative products and solutions
- ☐ Think strategically
- ☐ Learn to influence and negotiate effectively
- ☐ Be resourceful.

Four Tools to Effective Managing

Are you faced with managing others, but, like first-time parents, you're winging your way through the challenge? To spare your sub-ordinates from running the guinea pig wheel, memorize and practice the following basic skills:

- ☐ Develop people through feedback and coaching
- ☐ Create a positive work environment by encouraging inclusive-ness and brainstorming
- ☐ Communicate effectively with staff
- ☐ Define, direct and delegate work

Work often requires spending more time with your boss than with your own lover. Do yourself a favor: Pick a supervisor you click with and who generally supports you.

Foreplay for Fair Play:
Managing the Ethical (and Unethical) in Your Office Space

―――∽◦◦◦∾―――

"My company had just been acquired by another company, and I was flying to the big city of New York for my first time to meet with the new CEO. Our flirt came on like Donkey Kong almost from the get-go, despite that he was a good 14 years older than me, and, oh yeah, my new boss's boss. I naively became infatuated with him, the city, the new company, my perception of his position within the company, his intelligence, his charm, his persistence . . . you name it. It was all new to me, and I felt special! Long story short, a long-distance flirtation turned into a sexual relationship over the next five months. The thrill of the adventure increasingly grew into enormous anxiety when we faced plenty of 'almost-got-caught' moments by some of the other staff. Then our relationship ended almost overnight when I learned my CEO was actually a world-wide CE-HO! Turns out he had several flings in the making with other women at our company's international branches. Eventually, he was ousted from his

job and I somehow came out of it unscathed. I look back and think about how stupid it was to risk all that was important to me — my credibility, my reputation, my job and my mentor's respect — for a guy whom I'd known from the get-go I could never bring home to meet my parents!"
— Nancy, 32, Software Sales Representative

A Hip Girl's confidence is her greatest outward strength, but her true beauty is revealed when she exposes and accepts her shortcomings with grace. While we do our best to do what's best, sometimes our vulnerabilities cause us to make choices we would normally berate our own girlfriends for. So whether it's succumbing to your infatuation with the office cutie, or making a remark unknowingly offensive to a colleague, owning your mistakes and rectifying them is important. But not all situations come with instructions. In fact, most scenarios have more gray areas than clear solutions. So check out some of the more challenging work-related topics below for a starting point on what's appropriate behavior at your job.

Managing Diarrhea of the Mouth

Gossip doesn't resolve anything. Instead, it ignites a blazing fire of inaccuracies where there may be few sparks of truthfulness. But, like pimples we work hard to minimize, office gossip is unfortunately a fact of life. So how do you make office gossip work in your favor? Check out some of the different ways to handle what you're hearing.

◆ **Consider the source.** Does the person dispensing the information have the authority, expertise or credibility on the topic to be reliable? If not, perhaps it's not worth worrying about.

◆ **How does the information affect you?** You hear your colleague on the East Coast is resigning. Is her leaving going to create an opportunity for more work or advancement for you? If the gossip has a direct affect on you, you can take a moment to prepare in case the rumor is true. But until you hear it from the woman in charge, sit tight and quietly strategize your next career move in the event the information is accurate.

◆ **The gossip has little to do with you or your position.** Then just keep the rumors to yourself. Don't put yourself in the middle. Sometimes playing dumb to privy information is the smartest option: like when one of your best gals tells you a secret that one of your other gals had sworn you to secrecy about.

◆ **Minimize your alone time with the obvious gossip culprit.** The less you are within earshot of what she's spreading, the more you are able to focus on what's important in your job, and the less likely you can become a victim of her story-telling. Oftentimes, people who are incessantly spreading rumors don't have enough work of their own, or are insecure about their own role within the company structure.

◆ **Is the rumor about you?** If it is, weigh how damaging it is to your reputation. If it's a wildly ridiculous story about how you slept your way to the top, a story like that doesn't warrant a response. If the rumor is about the future of your position, perhaps you should consider dispelling the rumors of your departure because it's clearly shaking the morale of the department.

◆ **If you can't say something nice, don't say anything at all.** In this case, mom does know best. Plain and simple, resist the temptation to talk smack about your colleagues. Otherwise, your words can be twisted as they spiral through the rumor mill and come back to bite you in your J-Lo bootie.

Looking for Love (or Lust) in All the Wrong Places

You work eight hours (if you're lucky) a day with the same people. While we don't recommend you date anyone that you work with, the truth of the matter is that most of us will find one or two of our co-workers attractive at some juncture in our careers. Flirting with a colleague can be innocent fun, but you both have to be on the same page. And if you decide to take the leap and fish off the company pier, you'd better wear your life vest. Because when it comes to mixing "business" with "pleasure," don't forget there's a 50/50 chance that it may or may not work out in your favor. Here are some office romance factors to consider:

◆ **Know your company policy about dating colleagues.** Various organizations and businesses forbid it and might require a transfer, while others are more lenient and have minimal requirements about divulging it.

◆ **Be overly discreet about your office flirtations.** Don't flaunt your attraction in front of all your co-workers. Trust us, people can virtually smell the wild attraction from miles away and notice lingering eye contact, overly touchy-feely-ness, or giggly moments and frequent office-to-office visits. So no matter how good you think you're being about disguising your office romance, take extra precautions for keeping your office interactions minimal.

◆ **Using company email or instant messaging to say "I love you" is dangerous.** The computer support team generally has the right to traffic computer-related communication.

HipTip *If you insist on sending your office sweetie notes of hanky panky while at work, log onto your own Internet service email account. The like-*

lihood that it can be traced by your computer support team is minimal. Just don't leave your instant messaging up on screen when you make a quick dart to the restroom.

◆ **Dating more than one person at a time** from your job will give you a bad reputation within your company and may leave people seriously questioning your character. If you feel compelled to date another person from your office, allow some time (at least several months) after ending one work flirtation before courting another colleague.

◆ **Getting busy with the boss is very dicey.** As exhilarating as it might make you feel, rarely does it work out. In fact, you could end up losing your job and respect and gain a reputation of "sleeping your way to the top" that could easily follow you to your next gig. Now that's quite a gigantic mistake to overcome. Look at Monica Lewinski. She probably didn't plan for her relationship with Bill Clinton to pan out quite like it did. (See the "Safeguarding from Sexual Harassment" section for more on this.)

◆ **Keeping the work at the office is tricky.** You're kidding yourself if you don't think you'll vent about your colleagues with your work flirt. And if the relationship doesn't go quite the way you want it to, better hope your ex doesn't tell the office "flirt" how you really feel about her promiscuous behavior.

◆ **Whether you're in love or lust,** treating your office romance with the utmost respect is important. This isn't the relationship to play games with. Not returning calls, cheating or skipping town are sure-fire ways to gain a bad reputation with your colleagues.

Hip Tip *When it's possible, agree on a cordial response to tell your co-workers when they figure out that your romance has ended. And keep your new love lives out of the office. Otherwise, expect to hear all about his new flames through the rumor mill . . . and him to hear about yours.*

◆ **If you're the perpetrator of the break up,** better do it over a long weekend at home. You'll want the extra time for your partner (and you) to sort out feelings.

Hip Tip *Don't forget that even after the relationship has ended, you'll still have to see your former love day in and day out. Seeing him, no matter how badly you want to, is not going to make getting over the break-up any easier. Try to take a different route to the restroom instead of the way that forces you to pass by his cubicle. Use the phone or email to communicate work-related information . . . it makes the communication less personal. If push comes to shove, you may need to request a transfer. But whatever you do, don't "accidentally" stalk him. Desperation is never fashionable.*

Safeguarding Against Sexual Harassment

Sexual harassment is a very serious offense. Oftentimes, we women are the victims. But it's equally important to recognize that in today's world, a Hip Girl's sassy side can be easily construed as sexual harassment by some (like squeezing the office cutie's biceps as he kindly moves a box for you). Unfortunately, there are no hard and fast rules.

Check out some pointers below about how to handle your innocent urges to be "playfully" expressive at work.

Hip Tip *The Equal Employment Opportunity Commission (EEOC) defines two forms of sexual harassment. The first, "Quid Pro Quo Harassment," can be defined as: An employee who suffers a job detriment (e.g., a termination, demolion or loss of a promotion or raise) for refusing to accede to sexual demands is the victim of sexual harassment. This can also include the promise of a promotion, some sort of advancement or job loss. And remember, this includes not only your co-workers and bosses, but also your clients, customers and vendors. The second form of sexual harassment is "Hostile Work Environment." This is when an employer creates or allows an employee to repeatedly be subjected to unwelcome sexual conduct (comments, actions or both) to the point that the harassment unreasonably interferes with the employee's work performance or creates an intimidating, hostile or offensive working environment.*

◆ **Watch your language.** Skip using words from various sexual reproductive body parts in the office. Control your urge to call someone by a pet name like cutie, sweetie, doll or babe. Also, speak like a lady. (Save any naughty girl behavior for your bedside manner.) Be cautious of how you compliment your co-worker on his appearance.

◆ **Don't forward any sex-related jokes or pictures** via email or otherwise. Period.

◆ **Keep your hands to yourself.** Yes, you learned this rule in kindergarten, and it still holds true in the adult world. Your touchy-feely style of communication is most effective when dealing with friends and family members.

◆ **Don't show 'em everything you've got.** Be mindful of what you wear to work so as not to flaunt your "bare essentials" too much. (See the "Career Couture" chapter for more details.) While no sexual advances are justifiable at work, minimizing your chances of being "sexually objectified" can't hurt.

◆ **Don't ask for dates** or make sexual advances when it is clear, or becomes clear, that your admiration is unrequited. Get a clue. You want the guys at the bar to take a hike when you give them a polite brush-off. Recognize it when someone politely signals you to back off.

◆ **Accept a rejection** and don't retaliate if you're dissed. Sure it might be slightly embarrassing (which is why we don't recommend dating in the office), but skip the stalking. Don't leave notes or shoot off emails pushing your agenda in hopes of intimidating or changing your work flirt's mind. Just because he's not interested doesn't mean you're not good enough. For whatever reason, his cab light's not on. Your chances of getting where you want to go in a relationship is much higher with a guy whose cab light is shining brightly.

Standing Up Against Sex Invaders

Holding your own can be very unnerving when a co-worker or, worse yet, a boss makes you feel intimidated or uncomfortable because he "gropes" you with his eyes or hands or makes inappropriate sexual innuendos in the office or at after-hours meetings. Deflecting the attention of an unrequited admirer at work is a delicate matter. Here are a few suggestions for getting you through such a gut-wrenching experience:

◆ **Email.** Should you receive emails filled with sexual undertones or jokes — and you aren't comfortable with them — respectfully, but firmly, reply with an email asking the sender to not include you in such emails. Try, "Hey, Sam. This is pretty funny stuff, but to be honest with you, I don't feel comfortable receiving this kind of mail at work. So could you please take me off your distribution list for these sorts of sexually-explicit materials?" Save the emails for documentation in the event he disregards your request. If the perpetrator persists, tell him if he doesn't stop, you'll be forced to report it to your supervisor and HR. If he continues, don't mess around with idle threats. Take it to your boss and document it with your HR department in case it becomes a matter of his word against yours. And if you in any way fear for your safety from the very first email, take it directly to your boss and HR director. Your safety is of the utmost importance.

Hip Tip *Know your personal rights when you're faced with sexual harassment. Equal Rights Advocates (ERA) provides free legal advice and information about gender discrimination concerns in employment and education, including sexual harassment, pregnancy discrimination, family medical leave, pay equity and retaliation for complaints. The ERA Legal Advice and Counseling Hotline number is 800/839-4372, or visit their Website at www.equalrights.org.*

◆ **Verbal abuse.** If someone is persistent about asking you for dates (and you've made it clear you're not interested), their questions or comments about your personal life become intrusive, or he makes inappropriate statements about your body or appearance, don't waste another minute; consider taking your complaints to HR. Ultimately, you are the judge about what you can tolerate. And if you've made it clear to the advancer that you feel uncomfortable, don't worry about his comfort level. Take care of your feelings by not allowing it to recur without his facing repercussions. Sometimes we women become too concerned for the feelings of others and shove our feelings aside to accommodate others' comfort or happiness. Remember this: He's clearly not respecting your feelings. Don't worry about his.

◆ **Physical intrusion.** Should someone take it upon himself to touch you, block your movement, leer or make unwanted sexual gestures at the expense of your comfort level, once again, assess how comfortable you feel dealing with the situation yourself. If you feel confident that the first offense can be handled between the two of you without retaliation of some sort, that's your prerogative. But if you fear otherwise, take immediate measures to protect yourself and your status with the company by telling HR and your boss about the advances. Listen to your instincts and don't brush them off as invalid or overly sensitive. No one else can determine for you what you're feeling.

Hip Tip   *How you deal with unwelcome attention in any work-related environment (including at the office, on a business trip, in a hotel or restaurant, on a plane, playground, golf course or anywhere else you find yourself intermixing with potential and current business buddies) is ultimately up to you. Personally, this Hip Girl chooses to first attempt to deflect unwanted sexual attention by throwing the uncomfortable feeling back in his lap through sarcasm. Many others opt to be more direct, which, if you're one of them, you go girl! We hate to tell you that sometimes being able to delicately dance around the awkward advance is practically an unwritten rule for your success at many jobs. Sometimes, instead of immediately running to a boss or HR rep, side-stepping unwanted sexual advances or sexual "jokes" is often an unspoken preference in dealing with people at work who don't know where to draw the line. It can be an underlying skill that will help you be more successful at your job. But when push comes to shove, and your feelings, safety and dignity are on the line, remember you are the most precious commodity you have. Protect yourself first and foremost!*

◆ **Superior-subordinate power play.** This kind of manipulation is the worst. But sometimes falling for your boss is inevitable when he turns your respect for him and a vulnerable moment into an opportunity to score. If you find yourself in a relationship or a singular sexual encounter with your supervisor and you realize you aren't feeling good about your decision, don't beat yourself up. Many Hip Girls have found themselves in similarly vulnerable positions, like the story at the beginning of this chapter. But do get out of the relationship immediately and honestly by privately telling your boss in a public space, "I don't feel comfortable with this situation anymore and want to return to a strictly professional relationship." (As tempting as it may be, don't pull a Bridget Jones and ridicule your boss in front of all your colleagues.) If he pressures you into staying, or you fall victim to intimidation, report the incident and confess your relationship to your HR department. If you manage to end the courtship amicably, and you feel confident you haven't lost respect for him as a superior, and he's not retaliating by creating bad work conditions, then props to you. But it's equally honorable to request a transfer to another location or department or to take a job at an entirely different company to get yourself back on the right career path.

Hip Tip   *A corporation's Human Resources (HR) department serves numerous important employee-related functions. HR professionals serve as role models within the company for maintaining the highest level of standards and ethics. Lest we forget, they are human too. Therefore, do not be surprised if you come across some companies whose HR practices do not consistently adhere to sound HR protocol. But if you dutifully follow your company's harassment policy (or if there is none, report harassment to your HR team or boss when there is no HR office), it's your superior's legal responsibility to fully investigate your* claims. If you feel strongly that your HR department did not handle your particular situation properly, or in the case where your boss is the perpetrator and there is no HR team, consult an attorney about your rights.

Other Forms Of Discrimination

Sexual harassment isn't the only form of discrimination we women face in corporate America, or as waitresses, doctors, lawyers, actresses, teachers or flight attendants. Below are some additional areas of potential inappropriate behavior. We also encourage you to pick up additional materials on each if you are the victim of a predator at work.

◆ **Hip Girls come in all shapes, colors and sizes.** In the United States, where we are a melting pot of cultures and religions, we Hip Girls also practice our individualized religious and spiritual rituals. So if you feel you're the victim of discrimination based on your ethnicity, gender or religious practices, know that the United States law prohibits such actions. According to the Department of Labor, "The Civil Rights Act of 1964 prohibits discrimination in hiring, promotion, discharge, pay, fringe benefits, job training, classification, referral and other aspects of employment, on the basis of race, color, religion, sex or national origin."

HipTip *Reverse discrimination and so-called "quota" standards are unlawful. The law clearly prohibits discrimination in any form against any and all races, sexes, religions (or lack thereof) and so on. The EEOC is a division of the United States government established to enforce work force labor laws in this country. For more information on your rights, log onto www.eeoc.gov, or phone their toll-free number at 1-800-669-4000.*

◆ **Sexual orientation discrimination.** At the time of this printing, no federal law exists to protect people from being fired, refused work or otherwise discriminated against merely for being gay, lesbian or bisexual. There are now 13 states in the U.S. with anti-discrimination laws that offer some protection to the lesbian and gay community. There are, additionally, separate state, city and county civil rights ordinances across the country which have been adopted to cover lesbians and gay men in areas such as employment, public accommodations, housing, credit, union practices and education.

HipTip *At time of this printing, 15 states have anti-discrimination laws. Some apply in more areas than others. The laws in each state are constantly being amended. To find out the latest and greatest in your area, log onto www.lambdalegal.org*

◆ **Age discrimination.** Some professions, such as the business, medical, financial, legal and university worlds, respect the experience of a more mature Hip Girl, while other industries, such as the creative worlds of acting, web design, beauty and fashion, cater more to the younger Hip Girl demographic. Know which age range your world favors and work the system to your advantage. If you work in an environment where youth is cherished, appropriately play up your hip factor. But if you work in an industry that clearly embraces experience, then keep your colleagues and superiors guessing your age by letting your office etiquette and work ethic make them feel you have more years behind you than perhaps you truly do. The best insight we Hip Girls have to offer you regarding age: Don't reveal your age (or anything about your lifestyle that might announce it). It can be unfairly and unconsciously used against you.

The Age Discrimination in Employment Act (ADEA) of 1967 protects individuals who are 40 years of age or older from employment discrimination based on age. The ADEA's protections apply to both employees and job applicants. Under the ADEA, it is unlawful to discriminate against a person because of his or her age with respect to any term, condition or privilege of employment — including, but not limited to, hiring, firing, promotion, lay-off, compensation, benefits, job assignments and training.

◆ **Pregnancy discrimination.** If you're applying for a new job, and you are not visibly pregnant, you are not required to inform your potential employer of your health condition, just as you cannot be fired for becoming pregnant on the job. (An employer, however, can ask if you suffer from any condition that might impede your abilities to perform your job function successfully with reasonable accommodations.) The Family and Medical Leave Act (FMLA) entitles a covered employee to take up to 12 weeks of leave in a 12-month period for the birth or adoption of a child, or for taking care of a serious health condition of the employee or the employee's child, spouse or parent. Coverage is required by federal law if an employee has worked for his or her employer for at least 12 months or at least 1,250 hours during a 12-month period and is employed at a worksite where the employer employs at least 50 employees within a 75-mile radius. Some state laws may cover employers with fewer than 50 employees. Check with your regional Women's Bureau Office to see how your particular state laws can assist you. Log onto the Internet and use a search engine (like Google or AOL) to search your state and "Women's Labor Bureau" as key words to locate your local office. (To clarify: While the FMLA protects your right to take a leave, actual pay for time off during maternity leave falls under the Disability Leave Act.)

Hip Tip The U.S. Department of Labor Women's Bureau, established by Congress in 1920, is the only federal agency mandated to represent working women in the public policy process. Its mission is to promote the welfare of wage-earning women, improve their working conditions, increase their efficiency and advance their opportunities for profitability. You can get more information at www.dol.gov/wb.

Don't let your workspace work you over. Be proactive. Know your rights and exercise your own integrity when dealing with others.

The Big "O"—Opportunity:
Taking Charge of Your Career

—⟨⟩⟨⟩⟨⟩—

"A colleague-turned-friend and I had become complacent in our corporate travel jobs and wanted a new challenge, something that would feed our minds and free up our schedules to do the other things in life we enjoyed. And if we were going to be slaves to our work, we wanted it to be for something we felt proud of, instead of pushing someone else's passion. So we became business partners and, together, pooled our resources to open our own coffee shop business. Those first few years were scary and challenging, between meeting certain law requirements, finding vendors and dumping all our savings into our unknown futures. But our risk paid off, and we've even recently opened our second store."

—Salle, 32, Coffee Shop Owner

Nurturing Your Ambitious Spirit

In a perfect work world, employers will value and reward your strategic, productive and responsible skills. But when it comes to your career, don't automatically expect a fairy tale ending. We hate to break it to you so harshly, but you aren't Cinderella and this ain't a fairy tale existence. The chances that you'll be promoted on the merits of your efforts alone are slim. When you're working for someone else, you'll likely have to find your own opportunities for advancement. Just as you look for someone to date who has most of the qualities you're looking for in a mate — among them being flexible and supportive of your needs to grow as an individual — recognize a job and supervisor that offers the same.

In dating, you sometimes have to create your own opportunities for meeting — from positioning yourself next to the cutest guy in the bar to going to an art showing of an artist you adore. The same holds true in the workplace. This means you're likely going to have to take the first step in creating your own niche or opportunity for growth. To accomplish this, it's usually helpful to know at least your short-term goals. That's the best way to attain your long-term dreams. But sometimes we don't always know our direction. That's okay too. Sometimes the best adventures are those where the final destination is uncertain. You just need to know what direction to start heading.

Regardless of your situation, grab a pen and take charge of your immediate future by determining your upward mobility in your current situation.

Quiz One: Determining Your Upward Mobility

Whether you're already employed by a company or merely a prospective candidate, take a close look at the department and company as a whole and ask yourself the following questions to determine what your current opportunities might be for advancement.

1. **What's the department's employment loyalty ratio?**
   Is there heavy employee turnover or have people stayed for years and years? Measure the years of loyalty both for people at your level and several layers above you. This should give you a good indication if your company and management team promotes from within before looking outside of the company to recruit good help. Plus, if no one ever leaves and they have more seniority than you, ask yourself if there's any room for you to move up any time soon.

   Score 5 points if management is lean and if those who are in management positions have been promoted from within.

   Score 3 points if people have moved up slowly, balanced by other employees who came from the competition.

   Score 0 points if management is top heavy and if there's either heavy turnover of employees or if almost no one has been promoted in the last few years. Points _____

2. **What's the department's and company's financial forecast?**
   Have they had any recent layoffs? Is the company's stock surging or suffering from a serious nosedive? Is the boss tightening up office supply expenses and travel? Consider it a sign that there may not be enough bucks in the budget to build in a new position or promotion. But if you notice frivolous spending on dinners with clients, outrageous cell phone bills, or an influx of new equipment and employees, your financial future is looking brighter.

   Score 5 points if there's a healthy budget for your supplies and equipment or travel and expense reimbursements, a rise in employee head count, or if the company's stock has been on a steady rise to the top.

Score 3 points if the company's stock is steady, the resource budget is unchanging, or no positions have been added or dissolved.

Score 0 points if the company stock is rapidly declining, open positions aren't being filled, or budgets and resources are quickly freezing.

Points _____

3. **Take inventory of your and your department's workload.**
   Has your work responsibility increased substantially over a sustained period of time, or are you secretly shopping online and instant messaging friends just to make it look like you're busy all day long? Determining yours and your department's consistent workload can aid in deciding if a promotion is warranted or if business is looking leaner.

   Score 5 points if your workload is consistently increasing.

   Score 3 points if your work responsibility is steady, but unchanging.

   Score 0 points if four days out of the five-day work week you're playing hooky and no one is mentioning anything about you.

   Points _____

4. **Monitor your immediate colleagues' status.**
   Have any of them recently been promoted or let go? If so, identify as best you can how or why. Instead of just guessing or letting department gossip guide you, go straight to "the horse's mouth" (participating in the workforce rumor mill, after all, rarely offers honest, worthwhile information for your own career journey). Consider asking your boss what qualities or skills the department values or disapproves of — acknowledging that it's good information for strategizing your own growth in the department. If the lay-

offs were in masses, you can certainly be direct with your inquiry with your boss about what your future is with the company.

Score 5 points if there's a steady flow of people in your department moving up every couple of years or so.

Score 3 points if on rare occasion someone at your level is promoted.

Score 0 points if no one has been promoted within the last two to three years, or if more employees have left within that same timeframe.

Points _____

5. Identify promotion patterns within your department and company.

Have most of your colleagues been promoted after a relatively equal time of service? Did most of them earn a higher degree of education or certification before they received an increase in their paycheck? Did they hit a company quota or land a prized client? Do they belong to the same "clique" of people that seem to be moving ahead quickly? Were many of your colleagues recruited for another job by a competitor before securing more money from your company? A fair evaluation of what it takes others in your world to move ahead is an easy way to gauge what your company values. This empowers you to decide if you're interested in doing some of the same things to climb the professional ladder and if you fit the mold sculpted before you.

Score 5 points if you can clearly identify a promotion pattern and you feel confident you can meet those standards.

Score 3 points if the pattern appears less structured and you question the recognizable qualities valued.

Score 0 points if there seems to be no rhyme or reason behind someone being promoted or if the hardest working, most loyal employee is still making copies and faxing.

Points _____

6. **Evaluate your relationships within the structure.**

    Do you generally get along well with and feel respected by the people you work with, including colleagues, bosses and clients? Be honest with yourself. If you have a self-inflated view of how others perceive you, it could be enough reason not to promote you. See the "Building (Not Burning) Bridges" chapter.

    Score 5 points if you occasionally get both verbal and written (in email or review form) reinforcement from your boss, clients or colleagues, and if they come to you when they need something.

    Score 3 points if you only receive high rankings during company review time or parent-teacher conferences, or if your colleagues occasionally ask you to join them in lunches and social outings.

    Score 0 points if your boss, clients or colleagues consistently complain about you or resist supporting your needs, and if they rarely ask you to join them in meetings, off-hour activities or company-sponsored sports events.

Points _____

7. **Evaluate your flexibility.**

    Save your Downward Dog and back flips for your Yoga class. In this book, we're asking your flexibility in relation to your willingness to bend for your company. Gauge your commitment to extending yourself for your job. Are you willing to move departments, districts, grades or locations? Can you travel at the last minute, work longer hours or learn a new skill if a new position requires it?

If a company has a specific need and you repeatedly have limited flexibility in accommodating them, there's a good chance they'll look to someone else who can better suit their needs.

Score 5 points if your boss comes to you first or regularly to accommodate a last-minute tutoring session, extra shift or to spearhead a new project.

Score 3 points if you step up and take on extra work or travel only after everyone else in your department has gone into hiding.

Score 0 points if you're rarely asked to take on additional responsibility or if you've resorted to using your menstrual cycle as an excuse for missing the company-wide meeting.

Points _____

8. **Is there a role, position or department that interests you?**
Lest we not forget what matters most in your career, do something you enjoy and that you do well. Can you envision yourself with the department or company for another two to three years? Or does the thought of it depress you so much that you chow down on french fries or chocolate any chance you get to give you the pleasure that your job cannot? Do you see an arena in which there's room for growth for both you and your company? For instance, might there be a need for a full drama department at the university where you currently teach speech, or can you substantiate your proposal to open up a Midwest or international office (Hola, Barcelona! Here you come!)? Good for you for thinking strategically. Look in-house first to satisfy your thirst for more. If more people applied that same philosophy to their love lives, the divorce rate just might decrease. But if you're over it, and all looks like a dead end, perhaps moving on instead of up is best.

Score 5 points if you can pinpoint one or two titles, departments, or new lines of business brewing or that you have interest in learning more about.

Score 3 points if the opportunity isn't immediate but you foresee its formulating within the next year or two.

Score 0 points if nothing about your company, industry or department gets you excited about going to your job, except the free Krispy Kreme donuts on Fridays.

Points _____

9. Tally your total.

Total Points _____

Mover and Shaker (40-28 pts.)

Your chances of moving up and on within your department or organization look solid. The world is your oyster and in it is your pearl. So grab your pole and flip-flops, girl, it's time to go fishing. First determine at least your short-term career goals. Then strategize for the best bait to catch your oyster. Just remember: Persistence and patience are the makings of a top-notch fisherwoman.

Smooth Operator (27-15 pts.)

Okay, so if there's room to grow in your department or company, it's not knocking on your door loud enough for you to hear it. Better put your hard hat on; you're going to have to go drilling. Start by asking yourself some simple questions: Are some of the less optimistic answers from above re-workable or not a priority to you or your organization? Is there at least the possibility of meeting your short-term goals before moving on to reach your long-term accomplishments? Investigate and recognize what opportunities await and if you're interested in any of them. This will help you decide if you can strike it career rich right where you are or if you need to drill elsewhere before you strike oil. The good news is that you're in a position that offers several options. Just think long and hard about what your heart truly desires. Then strategize to make it happen.

Deal Breaker (14-0 pts.)

Is it time to face your reality and find a way to satiate your need for more responsibility? Or are you content to stay where you are while you work on balancing your personal happiness? Sometimes status quo ain't so bad if you're comfortable in your career, especially if there are other areas in your life that you need to pay more attention to (check out "The Great Balancing Act" chapter for more specifics). But if you find yourself stuck in a professional rut, snap out of it, girl, and grab the bull by the horns. Because after all, you can only fake an orgasm so many times before your partner notices. You can bet that if you're feeling unsatisfied in your job, it won't go undetected forever either.

Check Yourself: Where Do I Go from Here?

All righty, then. Now that you've considered your opportunity-for - advancement forecast, use the basic career tool kit below to map out your next professional path. After reading each option carefully, choose the one that best suits both your current situation and your desired direction. Tailor your choice to fit your style, just like you would break in, hem, nip or tuck even the nicest fitting pair of jeans before wearing them.

◆ **Departmental diva.** There's room to grow within your department, and you think you'd like to take the leap to the next level. Put your most comfortable dancing shoes on, ladies. A dance marathon just might be in your future. But formalizing a smart strategy will give you a better chance of winning. If you answer "Yes" to most of the questions below, and you still want to move up in your department, flip to the "Nailing the Negotiations" chapter to get started.

☐ You like your boss (and she likes you), and the two of you get along well enough to work alongside each other for at least another year or two.

☐ There are new areas or situations in which you can learn new skills, like a different area of the law, reporting on sports instead of politics or how to promote the record of an artist your company discovered.

☐ There's enough creativity in your job. If it's mainly paper flow and politics and you've got a creative urge, can you find a way to infuse your creative juices into your work? For instance, can you write the press releases instead of just pitching the stories for publicity, or can you try your hand at designing the front window display for your department's new fall clothing line?

☐ Do you think your department can reward you properly for your expertise and for taking on more responsibility? After all, what would be the point of having kids if the rewards didn't outweigh the years of inconvenience and exhaustion? Why should you suffer by taking on more work in a job, if in the end the company can't ante up on the benefits? If you think your company will try to short-change you in the exchange of work load and what you get out of it, you might need to consider securing an offer from the competition to get what you're after.

 Join an instant community of women you can access quickly at your fingertips. Log onto www.ivillage.com and punch in "work"

for live chats, articles and other related organizations that can help you get from your career what you're after and commiserate with you about your struggles.

◆ **Move over maven.** Is your Upward Mobility Score as lukewarm as your interest in the guy who actually let you buy him a drink? What? He doesn't know the old trick by now, that when you offer, you're just testing his chivalry? Well, ladies, just as we can't expect a man to predict our intentions, neither can we expect our bosses to predict our ambitions. If you think you might want to switch your role in the company, ask yourself some of the following questions first. Then skip to "Nailing the Negotiations" chapter to make your move.

☐ Is there a department or division you would like to move to where a position is currently open? Maybe you'd like to slide over to administration instead of teaching, or move from administering airline tickets to become a flight attendant or pilot?

☐ You like your potential new colleagues and think you could fit in with their department with relative ease. You don't always want to see them in the elevator and hear them gossiping about Donna's new scandalous love affair or the boss's wretched management style. Scout it out. These details are just as important in determining your potential happiness in a new division as the salary.

☐ Are there any benefits of your current position that you'll lose or gain if you transfer, and are they a priority to you? (For instance, will your pay decrease, your hours change drastically, your business travel increase or your body be more physically challenged? And what about your family? Will it affect their needs?)

☐ Will new responsibilities in a new position alleviate the responsibilities you dislike in your old position?

☐ Will a move help your ultimate goal? For instance, if you move from the marketing department as an assistant to the finance department because the title and pay is better, will that really help you in the long run if your ambition is to be the mastermind behind the next Budweiser advertisement campaign?

☐ Do you or can you meet the educational or skill requirements?

◆ **Visionary vixen.** You like your company and the people you work with, but you're tired of doing the same job, and none of the other departments appeal to you. Why not wow your bosses with your Hip Girl ingenuity by identifying a niche, division or area of expertise that the company isn't maximizing? With the right plan, you could be on your way to heading up a whole new after-school program or a multi-billion-dollar-grossing consumer products division.

☐ Do you feel passionate about your company's or institution's ultimate mission? If you can't quite get behind their goal to become the number one party destination because you're more interested in helping raise the profile of a leukemia organization, then what's the point in starting up a whole new division — unless, of course, the experience will help you as a volunteer at the leukemia foundation.

☐ Do you think your company is open enough to listen to your idea? As you gather support (See "Nailing the Negotiations" chapter for more), it's just as important for you to make sure you are in a position for the right person to hear ya. For instance, if you're working in the mailroom and you have no access to the senior vice president — or his assistant — then you'd better have a plan to meet him. Or if your company has made it clear repeatedly that they aren't interested in developing a women's line of prophylactics and you can't substantiate with proof why they're missing an opportunity to make some serious money, then maybe you're better off ditching the company or starting your own business.

□   Why exactly do you want to take on this responsibility? Just make sure it's for reasons you'll find fulfilling.

□   While your homework should be a good indication to your company or institution that your idea will work for them, are you convinced you are the right person to make it happen? We all face self doubt, but as long as you know your facts, have some solid credibility and expertise in the field, and are dedicated to seeing it through, then selling yourself should be the easiest part of selling the idea. Just make sure you want to be part of the package deal when marketing it.

◆ **Entrepreneurial empress.** We've all shopped at stores or eaten at restaurants where we are certain that if we were the owners, the service, ambience or product would be much better. If you feel that impassioned about something — whether it's your current line of business, dancing, cars, rock climbing, sewing, rearing kids or taking pictures — why not consider starting your own business? You already know the basics from way back when you opened your first lemonade stand. Ask yourself some of the questions below. If you still think it feels right, then embrace your entrepreneurial spirit and take a calculated risk.

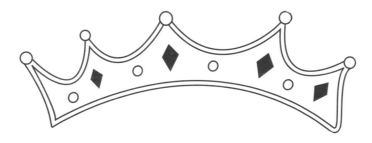

Hip Tip *The book* THE GIRL'S GUIDE TO STARTING YOUR OWN BUSINESS: CANDID ADVICE, FRANK TALK, AND TRUE STORIES FOR THE SUCCESSFUL ENTREPRENEUR *by Caitlin Friedman and Kimberly Yorio offers great tips, resources and formulas for getting your own gig running without reading like a boring business manual.*

- Are you prepared to work longer days and on weekends? Getting started in your own business could mean less time for mindless entertainment.
- Can you support yourself financially until you hit it big? That might mean your fancy lifestyle of jet-setting internationally will have to take a backseat.
- Do you have enough relationships and expertise to supply you with a small, but mighty built-in client roster?
- Will you have access to enough resources to maintain your needs, like office equipment, transportation, an assistant or cell phone?
- List exactly what it is about working for others (whether it's your current boss or a potential new employer) that makes you want to be your own boss. Is it the commute, or do they lack a risk-taking spirit? Do you disagree with the company's philosophy on business or their management style? Are there reasons enough for you to strike out on your own, or can you propose a compromise on some of them at your job? Or find what you're looking for at a new establishment?
- Can you find another way to supplement your benefits, like adding to your retirement fund or paying for your health insurance?

◆ **Cool and content Cathy.** Ambition is a quality that most bosses admire. But knowing when and how to apply it will surely make you score. If you ask for too much too soon, what you perceive as ambition might be construed by your boss and colleagues as an obnoxious sense of entitlement. Moreover, perhaps your brain has been in career overdrive for far too long, and for the sake of your sanity, you need to slow down. Ask yourself some of the questions below to help you decide if you should stay put and become an expert right where you are while giving more time to increasing your happiness in other areas of your life.

☐ Are you content or complacent? To put it simply: To be content means you're satisfied; to be complacent means you're tolerant of the situation. It's important to be clear on the difference. Cinderella was not satisfied as the ragged, belittled sister with no life. But Cinderella was complacent in her role, because she'd grudgingly accepted that this was her destiny and lost all hope. (Until, of course, along came a fairy godmother and a prince who saved her from her misery. Guess that's why it's called a fairy tale, ladies.)

☐ Have you been in your current position for a while (in terms of your company standards)? Demanding too much too soon could be construed as greedy and becoming too big for your britches.

☐ Are you still learning new skills or can you do your job blindfolded with both your hands tied behind your back while jumping up and down on a trampoline in an auditorium filled with a thousand screaming kids? (Okay, you get the picture.)

☐ Are there other professional career goals you'd like to achieve that you can accomplish in your current position, like earning your master's or doctoral degree, writing a novel, working as a weekend photographer's assistant, becoming a yoga instructor or training for the Olympics? Sometimes holding onto a position that's a no-brainer for you to do well and that you can still find enough enjoyment in doing is worth hanging in there while you pursue other aspirations.

❑   Are you fulfilled in your personal life? Would you like to go on an African safari with your friends or learn to speak Italian? Maybe now is the time to concentrate on the things in life you've put on hold. Perhaps now is the time to remodel your home, head up your kids' soccer team, or plan your wedding instead of taking on additional responsibility at work or learning a whole new work environment. If your current job doesn't allow you the time to do the more personally satisfying things in life, would another job or career offer more free time to spend nurturing the other things (or people) you love? (Read "The Great Balancing Act" for more information.)

❑   Do you have any family emergencies or obligations that you need to devote some serious time to? Perhaps one of your elderly parents needs more attention than usual. Or maybe your partner is in need of your business savvy for a while to get his landscaping business moving. Hip Girls realize that in helping others, sometimes we learn more valuable life lessons about ourselves or even new passions we never knew we had. Then later, when we can afford to be more selfish with our time, we can apply our newfound life lessons to our own ambitions.

❑   Are you overly stressed? If you find your current workload already exhausting, why overload yourself unnecessarily? Check out "The Great Balancing Act" for more on that.

◆ **Graduate goddess.** Whether you've been pondering a career change for a while, your profession requires a degree, or you just need a break from reality, pursuing your bachelor's, master's or Ph.D. can offer several benefits. But before you dive in, don't forget that there are several factors to consider. Read on and ask yourself a few of the questions below before turning to the "What Now?" chapter at the front of this book for more information about furthering your education.

- Is it your choice to go back to school? Are you trying to achieve a personal goal? Ultimately, you have to want to get your degree, even if your job is the catalyst. So make sure it's worth it to you in the end.

- Can you finance your education or find support for it?

- Your current lifestyle may be difficult to uphold if you go back to school. If you had to downgrade your living quarters, social activities or car, could you do it and still feel happy about your choice?

- Will the additional education benefit you personally and in your career once you finish?

- Is there anyone else you need to consult prior to working out details of your class load? A husband or boss might be directly affected by your extra-curricular responsibilities. It's only fair, and smart, that you try to get emotional support from the people who are in a position to make your conquest a more pleasant experience, because along with school comes additional stress. You just might need them to be more patient and understanding of your needs.

◆ **See ya sister.** You haven't felt this disrespected and unappreciated since your best friend ditched you for her new, soon-to-be ex-boyfriend. Or has the whole criminal court process lost its luster and left you longing to be a part of a more soul-rewarding career like teaching or working for a non-profit organization? If all signs point to little or no room for growth either in your department or within your company and you desperately want more responsibility, it's best if you start looking for another job opportunity. Don't sweat it. Sometimes the worst-case scenarios give us the courage we need to follow our hearts. After factoring life's little challenges into your equation, why not take a calculated adventure for the sake of personal gratification? But before making any rash decisions, read the following sections and chapters of this book:

- □ "Entreprenuerial Empress" (above)
- □ "Resigning: Off to Greener Pastures"
- □ "The Basics"

━━◅◖◗▻━━

Opportunities abound in life, and it's up to each of us to find ours. Figure out what opportunities you'd like to create for yourself, and the universe will conspire to help you achieve them!

PART THREE

———∽∾∿∾∽———

Get a Clue & Get a Life

Have you spent the last decade pursuing your career aspirations, virtually suffocating your personal happiness? Did you become the latest victim of a corporate downsizing and are you wondering what your future holds? Or, perhaps you wonder if you quit your job whether you'll find your personal pot of gold (and maybe even a cute leprechaun too) at the other end of the rainbow. Our "Get a Clue & Get a Life" section helps you navigate and juggle work-related life topics with style, grace and confidence.

What Now?

College, Trade School, Graduate Degree, Work or Bust

—◦◦◦—

"I landed a good job with great benefits right after college as a photo assistant. But, I never quite felt fulfilled. I secretly yearned to write for an entertainment or lifestyle magazine instead. But no matter how many contacts I made at the various well-known magazines, and the fact that I was willing to start at the entry-level position, I always heard the same story: 'We need someone with experience.' UGH! I mean, who knew I needed experience to answer someone's phone!? Frustrated with my desolate prospects, I took a leap of faith, and at age 25 enrolled in a New York journalism graduate school to be near the epicenter of the magazine world. It was the best decision I've ever made. After interning at YM and IN STYLE magazines and freelancing for the U.S. OPEN's Website, I landed my first full-time gig as an assistant editor, and I'm loving every minute of it."

— Rachel, 27, Entertainment Magazine Assistant Editor

ou've heard it before, and it's proven true time and time again: When one door closes, another one opens. The question isn't if you open the door, rather, which door you choose. So whether you're considering tackling graduate school while busting your butt at your corporate gig by day, switching fields or heading back to school for your undergraduate degree, deciding your next career move is nerve-racking but exhilarating. Read below to help you figure out which path you might want to consider next, no matter where you currently are in pursuing and fulfilling your career path.

Heading Back to School

Do you know which direction you want your career path to take? Or are you still ambivalent about what your future might look like? Here are some not-so-obvious reasons to seriously consider earning your undergraduate degree.

◆ **Most companies and professions in today's world** require employees to be college-educated.

◆ **You can test the waters.** If you're still undecided about what field you want to pursue, college offers courses in various fields to explore before fully committing to one specific career path. It also allows you to comfortably switch fields if you're not feeling so passionate about your current path.

◆ **Super-size your social skills.** If you sit quietly at the back of the boardroom while your more boisterous colleagues take the spotlight, or your manager's review suggests you need work on your customer service relations, perhaps you should consider an education in socializing. College offers a plethora of opportunities to build, practice and nurture the invaluable ability to meet and relate to other people. From joining student associations of professional organizations (like in marketing, public relations, hotel and restaurant management) to taking a speech class, joining a sorority or recreational soccer team, or simply living in a dormitory, you can beef up on your social networking and presentational skills.

◆ **Learn to love the "different."** Culture and travel opportunities abound at college institutions. Most universities offer domestic and international semester exchanges. If you've always dreamt about how people halfway across the world or country live, but your company can't get you a visa to work in their Spain division, or you can't afford to relocate to another state without a job, earning your college degree just might be your ticket. Beyond experiencing a whole new way of life, few things will help a person grow more than beginning all over in foreign territory. Additionally, colleges typically serve as a centralized spot for people of all backgrounds, ethnicities, religions and experiences to flock.

◆ **Network.** Most companies recruit at local universities and colleges for employees and interns because they serve as a mecca for potential. Also, instructors often have connections in the community, and your sorority or alumni association can often be used to establish an instant common ground.

◆ **Safe escape.** Looking for a quick way out of the small town where everyone knows your business or to get away from your overbearing parents? Perhaps you're tired of big-city living and want to experience what it's like to know your neighbors? College is a great and safe way to explore new ground without risking too much security.

U-bound or Community College Calling

Is getting your associate's degree worth your time, or should you enroll straight into a four-year educational institution? (Committing to a two-year college is like dating; you get to see what's out there without committing too much of your money or energy. A four-year institution is more like having a live-in boyfriend. While you can always change your mind, bailing isn't as easy; there's the division of property, finding a new home and reestablishing your independent living.) The answer lies within what your more immediate needs are and what your ultimate goals are. Check out below for more on which might serve you better.

Consider a Community College

◆ **Stretch that dollar.** If money is an issue, community college tuitions are usually only a fraction of the cost of attending a four-year university.

◆ **Tap your talent without breaking your bank.** You're not sure you're college material, or you're not content with your current career. Community colleges are an inexpensive way to get your feet wet. It'll give you a taste of what the university coursework will be like and allow you to try out various elected courses of interest before investing a whole lot of time and money to discover that recreational therapy or accounting isn't your thing.

Hip Tip *Transferring into most colleges as a junior is easier than being accepted as a freshman applicant. You'll get the same degree as the students who started there their first year. Plus, no one ever asks where you attended college your first two years. It's all about where you graduated from.*

◆ **Be a Rudy.** Like in the movie *Rudy*, don't let your high school grades or SAT scores hold you back from achieving your big U dreams. Let community college serve as your first step to making your dreams come alive. Get those dreadful general education courses — like accounting, speech, English or economics — out of the way by taking them in a more intimate setting. Community college classes are smaller and you can get more one-on-one help from the instructors. (This personal attention is especially important if you've got outside factors affecting your school experience, like kids or a job.)

◆ **Home is where your heart is.** Perhaps you need your parents' support to watch your kids while you're in class, or you're not ready to move two hours away or halfway across the country from your hometown honey. That's okay. Every Hip Girl flies at her own pace. Community college is a great way to stay near your support system and still kick off a college education. If you live at home, it's another great way to save on the cash flow. We say, if this is an option you've decided to take, milk that system until you're ready to take that leap of faith.

◆ **Be a big fish in a small pond.** Did your aspirations to play college ball fade quickly when you realized you got more time warming up the bench than strutting your stuff courtside? Sometimes being a big fish in a small pond is more rewarding, because you get more of a chance to shine. Less competition offers more opportunity for practice. And that extra year or two of experience just might be what you need to be the big girl on the university campus.

◆ **Scholarship opportunities.** Girl, free money is free money. Sometimes at the local level, your chance to get a scholarship is a little better with fewer competitors. Don't completely discount a community college until you've weighed all the pros and cons of your decision, particularly if you have the chance to charge your first two years of college on someone else's dollar.

◆ **Out-of-state tuition becomes more affordable.** Since junior colleges are less expensive all the way around, you can establish residency in another state far cheaper by enrolling in a community college first. Transferring to the university of your choice in the state you have residency allows you to get your undergraduate degree for less money. It is also less of a hassle. Consider that many in-state junior colleges create their associate's degree programs to complement the same state's university offerings. This makes it easier for students to transfer their credits from one college to another.

U-bound

◆ **Bridge building.** Going straight to a four-year university is a great way to build a foundation for your tight-knit community for the next four years. You can cement your social and networking circles earlier in your college career by living in dormitories, joining a sorority, or working and interning in the community where you hope to secure a job after graduation.

HipTip *Apply to a minimum of three colleges. Include a dream school (one you'd love to attend but your chances are up in the air), a good prospect (a place you'd like to attend, and where your grades and scores meet the requirements) and a safety (a college where you're sure your numbers will make you a shoo-in). Remember, each application requires a sizeable fee, so put some thought into where you want to go before applying anywhere.*

◆ **More opportunities to grow earlier in your college career.** If you transfer from a junior college to a university with too many credits, you may be passing up opportunities for semester exchanges abroad or getting in on the good university jobs like resident assistant.

◆ **Going straight to a university alleviates transfer issues.** Transferring from one college to another — whether from a community college or another out-of-state university — can sometimes present challenges. Some of your credits might not meet the university's standards, thereby requiring you to take more classes in algebra when you dreaded it (and nearly bombed it) the first time around.

◆ **Small fish in a big pond.** Have your fashion needs outgrown the local mall, or do you like immersing yourself in new environments and sinking or swimming on your own? Fewer comfort zones practically force you to "find yourself" and help you see that we Hip Girls are made of more than just sugar and spice. Going straight to a four-year university often requires a Hip Girl to mature a little faster because she has to learn to be more independent and resourceful. Yes, that means no more dad-runs to unclog your garbage disposal. Grab your copy of the *Hip Girl's Handbook for Home, Car and Money Stuff* instead.

◆ **Have your cake and eat it too.** You know how sometimes you want the comforts of a relationship, but you miss the thrill and infatuation stage of meeting new dating candidates and falling in love all over again? The beauty of enrolling in a university is that it doesn't negate you from taking junior college courses. You can have the best of both worlds. Take your more difficult general education courses at the junior level during your summer or holiday breaks from the university. It'll be cheaper and can speed up your graduation date. Just make sure the credits transfer properly.

◆ **Stiffer competition.** If you compare yourself to or compete against people who are as talented or skilled as you, you'll always look good. But if you really want to improve your game — whether as a basketball player, actress or math wizard — then "playing" amongst the "big-timers" can help push you to reach your fullest potential.

Trade School or Certification Courses

Perhaps committing to a two- or four-year education just isn't your style. But you do want to build your career on a foundation of solid skill and background. There are plenty of career choices that don't require typical college fare but do require that you be trained by professionals or certified by passing exams in such areas as hairdressing, auto mechanics, insurance, fashion design, electrical work, realty, massage, personal training or tattoo art. Trade school and certification courses, when paired with experience, can offer a strong partnership for succeeding in your chosen profession.

◆ **Certification programs often let you work more independently.** You pay for the materials and work at your own pace. Usually, you get several date options to take the exams for the course. So, study days and times become your choice.

◆ **Trade school and certification courses are specific to the field you're entering.** Skip those painful general education-required classes you were dreading. And don't waste your money and energy on "underwater basket weaving" when it doesn't apply to your future as a realtor or police officer.

Hip Tip *Check out the following Websites for more information about trade school programs and who offers them: www.trade-schools.net and www.careeradvantage.org.*

◆ **Class size is smaller** in trade schools. You get more one-on-one attention.

◆ **Hands-on learning.** Because trade schools are all about preparing you for one specific type of career, they're designed to incorporate real world experience into your curriculum.

◆ **Money factor.** Because there are fewer overhead costs to cover than at typical colleges where they have to upkeep dorms, massive classrooms and staff, trade school and certification program over-head costs are much less. This savings filters to you. Can you say "No exorbitant tuition fee"? Yeah, we figured that would catch your attention.

Hip Tip *Most colleges or universities offer continuing education courses in a variety of different genres, from corporate and professional programs and computer technology training to classes for teachers. These courses can be helpful in such areas as renewing your dental hygiene license or assisting in your salary advancements. Check with your local college or university to see what classes are offered and if they might be right for you.*

◆**Coming to a home near you.** Whether you have a family of your own to consider, or you're not quite ready to give up mom's secret meatloaf recipe, trade schools tend to be more accessible because they're conveniently located in all major cities and states. And the beauty of many certification programs is that you can do your work in your Hello Kitty pj's.

Working Stiff

Did you just graduate and you're wondering if jumping into the work world is for you? Or maybe you're a junior in college and your internship supervisor has offered to hire you. While we definitely advocate more education, we recognize and respect that some opportunities are too good to pass up and that formalized schooling isn't the generic answer for everybody's path to success. Here are a few reasons that working may be more your thing:

◆ **Your career path doesn't necessarily require it.** Professional experience in many fields is preferred. Getting the experience you need typically requires you to pass your trade school boards or at least be enrolled in school. But if you've persisted and stumbled upon an opportunity without having a formal education, you may want to think about your ultimate career goal. Will you need more education to get beyond the immediate opening?

◆ **You want to save up** to pay for as much of your education up-front as possible. That's truly admirable. Just make sure to give yourself a deadline and reevaluate your goal markers to check that you're meeting the milestones you'd set to get to college. Trust us, once you get used to a certain income level, cutting back to attend law school can be difficult (that means fewer new Banana Republic summer dresses or skipping the after-hours social and gossip sessions every so often).

Hip Tip *Money should never be a justification for not pursuing a higher education. Check out www.collegeboard.com for scholarships that might apply to you. Also, the federal government offers grants and loans. Log onto http://studentaid.ed.gov or www.students.gov to find out more. You should also speak to a college admittance and career counselor at a school near you.*

◆ **Your employer will pay for your education.** Okay, we've got to say that this one makes the most sense of all. If your current employer covers most or all of your college education, yeah, that's quite a deal you've got going. In most situations, that will require you to sign on with them for a several-year commitment. Plus, you'd better make sure you have a very strong self-motivating personality. Sometimes after a full day of playing executive babysitter or dealing with cranky customers, sitting in a three-hour class explicating Hemingway's work sounds as appealing as getting a Brazilian bikini wax. Youch!

◆ **Get a jump-start on networking** and building your reputation in your field. If you've got a personality and work ethic that stands out from the rest, work those assets by putting them to the test. But in order to make yourself indispensable to your company — 'cuz girl, let us tell you, there's no such thing as company loyalty any more — better make sure your competitors hear about your work too.

Hip Tip *Some easy ways to saturate your field and keep your name top of mind for a bigger, better deal is to join professional associations, engage in work-related social gatherings and volunteer for organizations that bring you, your colleagues and competitors together for a greater cause. Simply put: Get involved. The more people you know, the more opportunities you'll have to grow.*

◆ **You suffer from a serious anxiety or attention disorder.** The truth is, if you do, seek professional help. Perhaps a counselor or therapist can help you curtail it enough to attend college. But if just thinking about the restrictions and confinement of schooling is enough to have you praying to the porcelain god, then perhaps you should skip it. While the beauty of college is that it's less structured than K-12, it often requires you to follow instructions and sit in on some long, boring lectures. We get that some of you would rather listen to your parents try to explain sex to you all over again. You decide what your tolerance level is for spending five hours a day on material that may or may not get you excited.

◆ **You've been bitten by the travel bug.** We say, go girl! Do it while you have few restraints! Because if you're single, you've got fewer people's feelings to consider. And once you land that important 9-to-5 gig, your vacation time to explore will be much more limited. So, if you're putting off a more formal education for a year to pursue real world schooling or a spot on MTV's "Real World" television show, we applaud your gumption. Whether you're waiting tables, bartending in New Zealand or signing on to Nanny in Europe, you rock! Way to take charge of the life you want instead of just taking the route your friends or parents expect. Just be mindful to have a plan for your career before that year or two abroad comes to an end.

Hip Tip *Keep in mind that beyond a certain age, typically 24, most countries require a company to sponsor your move abroad. Check the laws in the countries you want to explore for more specifics.*

◆ **Others depend on your income.** While it's difficult, you can work part time and attend school full time or vice versa. But if you find yourself in a financial pickle and you have children or a husband who also depend on your income, you may need to devise a plan that puts your family's needs first.

Graduate or Ph.D. Degree

Are you considering going back to school to pursue your master's in business so you can open your own shop after spending the past 10 years pushing someone else's vision? Or are you fresh off the under-grad boat and aren't so sure you're ready to let go of the educational security blanket? There are plenty of reasons to consider enrolling in graduate school. Here are a few to help you to determine if the short-term agony of taking the GRE, LSAT or writing that dreadful thesis is worth your long-term happiness.

◆ **Your company or profession requires a higher degree to move ahead.** If your goal is to be Chief Financial Officer (CFO) someday, or if you want to be a doctor, teacher, principal or college professor, pursuing a degree beyond your bachelor's is likely a requirement.

◆ **You love learning.** So maybe your career path doesn't require a higher education, but perhaps you've been at your job for a while, and you're finding little room to grow in your department. If you already have a college degree, enrolling in graduate school can feed your need to expand your horizons and put you in an environment with people who share your passion for learning.

◆ **You become stiffer competition.** If you're competing for the same job against someone with the same amount of professional experience, a graduate degree may be the one leg up you might need.

◆ **Moneymaker.** With a master's or Ph.D., you can often request a higher salary. Now that can't hurt your quality of life, can it?

HipTip *Ask professionals in your field if earning your master's or Ph.D. before getting real world experience will work against you. Some professions or unusual situations — like statewide budget cuts or union-related issues — just might pass you up because they see you as too costly or too educated for the position available.*

◆ **What else are you gonna do?** Can't find a job post college? Perhaps you were part of a massive nationwide layoff and ain't nobody hiring.

Well, perhaps now is the time to stop procrastinating and go after your dream of earning your master's or Ph.D.

◆ **Musical careers.** Are you simply done with your Hollywood aspirations and ready to pursue your dreams of becoming a psychologist? Oftentimes, breaking into a totally new field is really difficult if you've spent a decade creating a niche in another field. Graduate school can help open a brand-new door that otherwise wouldn't be open for you to explore.

◆ **Master procrastinator.** Earning your master's or Ph.D. isn't important to your career success, but maybe it's important to your personal happiness. Should you earn your degree right after your bachelor's or master's, or are you certain you can make time for it even with the responsibilities of a full-time job, kids or a mortgage payment? Weigh your priorities. At the end of the day, your priorities are what matter.

Part-time or Full-time Student

You want to earn your college or post-graduate degree, but you're not sure if you want to head back to school full time or hit the work force and do the night school option. Here are just a few factors to consider:

◆ **Half the workload, double the time.** As a part-time student, you can balance your job and finances more easily. But earning your degree part-time will take you twice as long than if you dumped your day job and hit the books full-force. (Hey, at least your bank account won't suffer the consequences as much.)

◆ **Full-time student, half the lifestyle.** Unless you're a real-life Suze Orman and have saved enough to pursue the lifestyle you've grown accustomed to (or your daddy's last name is Hilton, Hilfiger or Trump), be prepared to make some serious cutbacks in your living habits like eating out, spontaneous girl trips to Palm Springs or the Hamptons, shoe-shopping sprees or roommate-free living. Know these cutbacks won't last forever, just long enough to get you through the next two or four years while you do your residency or pursue your doctorate.

Hip Tip *As we mentioned before, check out if your company will help you pay for your college education. There's no policy written on it? Perhaps you can negotiate it if they really want to keep you as an employee.*

◆ **Say adios to your personal time.** We hate to sound so dramatic, but if you're going to go back to school part-time, there's a slim chance that you'll have much of a life outside your full-time mommy duties, part-time night classes and all-weekend homework studies. And if you don't have a very understanding family and circle of friends to help you out around the house, you can forget about getting any real sleep for the next few years.

◆ **The ref might call interference if you choose to work** while going to college. No, we're not talking about football. We mean your big hon-cho. Your boss might need you to work late on a project despite the fact that you've got a big presentation or paper due at school. You better figure out how supportive your company and direct report will be of your higher education pursuits before you commit.

◆ **Ask yourself:** Are you going back to school solely to earn your degree or are you subconsciously yearning to live the carefree lifestyle? Your answer might help you solidify your decision. And remember, just because you start part time (or vice versa) doesn't mean you can't change your mind mid-way through your journey.

Life is a Sunday brunch buffet. Pick and choose what appeals to you, and go back as many times as you like until you have completely satisfied your appetite.

The Great Balancing Act:
Juggling Your Job and Your Personal Life

"I worked several years as a medical assistant, but when my husband's construction business took off, it put us in a position to live comfortably off his income (albeit not like royalty). So we agreed I'd stay home to raise our children. At first I struggled with my identity and my contribution to our family, the world and, most importantly — to me! Even with two adorable kids who demanded and deserved my attention, I needed to nurture my soul. I began taking photography courses and started assisting a wedding photographer whenever it worked into my schedule. I wasn't on a timetable, rushing to make it to the next level. I just pursued my hobby in between swimming lessons and playing classroom helper. Now I feel like I have the best of both worlds! I love being a full-time mommy and supportive wife and feel fortunate to have found a job I truly enjoy."

— Lorie, 32, Full-time Mom and Part-time
Wedding Photographer

Establishing our own identities and taking care of ourselves are the critical first steps in building the life of a Hip Girl. Work is often a place where we can find some satisfaction and purpose in our lives. But few of us can find ultimate happiness in our work alone (that's like saying our partners can fulfill our marathon-shopping sessions when only our girls will do!). Despite loving your role as a mother, teacher, wife, waitress, doctor, lawyer or housekeeper, know that you can't ever truly be happy if you define yourself only that way. Focus on building a well-rounded you: Do the things in life that help you become the best YOU! Check out some tips below for successfully and happily walking the tightrope of life.

Be a Super You, Not a Super Hero

Give yourself a break. A perfect balance among all parts of a well-rounded Hip Girl cannot be attained at all times. There will be times when certain areas of your life will demand more attention, meaning that less time can be focused on the other areas tugging at you — from getting your groove on with your single girlfriends, to doing the married couple thing, or finding a new passion in cooking, painting or surfing. But we're not suggesting that you ever neglect your husband, children, friends, job, hobbies or religion! In fact, sacrificing or compromising now doesn't mean you have to give up that trip to South Africa forever. We're simply saying to get your priorities in check and balance them. Then once you've accomplished that, re-evaluate your heart's yearning. Here's how to get started:

◆ **Think about where you were two years ago.** Perhaps you were pulling all-night study sessions to receive your college diploma. Maybe you had just given birth to your first child or were lobbying for a promotion to manager. Whatever goal you were striving for, check yourself: Did you accomplish it and are you satisfied with the progress you've made with your achievement?

◆ **Chart your new priorities.** Look at your life today and ask, "With all the great things I've accomplished, what part of my life is feeling unfulfilled at this very moment?" Maybe you want to find someone to share your life with or you're ready for children. The answer could be as simple as you want to see the world, give back through volunteering or get your body into killer shape. Or maybe you're finally ready to stop putting off the dreams of writing a book or opening your own cafe. Be honest with yourself. It may be one of the most difficult questions you'll ever face. But acknowledging what your heart's missing is the first step in finding it. Here is a small list of areas for you to consider. Weigh what areas you want to cultivate most now:

Family	____%
Friendships	____%
Love Life	____%
Hobbies	____%
Work	____%
Travel	____%
Volunteering	____%
Religion/Spirituality	____%
Graduate School	____%
Reading	____%
Relaxing/Sleeping	____%
Health/Exercise	____%
Other	____%
TOTAL	100%

Hip Tip   *Don't waste another minute. Read the book* MIDLIFE CRISIS AT 30 *by Lia Macko and Kerry Rubin* BEFORE *you turn 30. The authors researched the lives of Generation X & Y women in the workplace and life. To sum up their findings, generally speaking, Gen X/Y women were raised to focus on themselves and their careers first, and marriage and their personal lives later. Generation X/Y women who followed this advice found themselves in a "crunch period" approaching and shortly after turning 30 when they realized the other half of their lives had been ignored (with some new pressures of biological deadlines, despite that women are having babies later in life). Interestingly, their research also found that while the initial sentiment of Gen X/Y men was that they wanted a spouse who is "successful," "accomplished" and "an equal partner," men ultimately throw up self-protective shields when they sense potential neglect from a woman who's independent and prosperous. Why? Because man has believed from the beginning that he provides independence and a woman provides intimacy. Go figure.*

◆ Now look at the current make-up of your day and determine how you actually spend it. Keep a log for a week or two to help you gauge it better. For example:

Monday	6:30 a.m.–8:00 a.m.	Group yoga
	8:00 a.m.–9:00 a.m.	Got ready
	9:00 a.m.–10:00 a.m.	Commuted to work
	10:00 a.m.–1:00 p.m.	Worked
	1:00 p.m.–2:00 p.m.	Lunched solo
	2:00 p.m.–6:30 p.m.	Worked
	6:30 p.m.–7:30 p.m.	Commuted home
	7:30 p.m.–8:30 p.m.	Made dinner/ate at home solo
	8:30 p.m.–9:30 p.m.	Washed laundry
	9:30 p.m.–10:30 p.m.	Watched TV

10:30 p.m.–11:30 p.m.	Read
11:30 p.m.–6:30 a.m.	Slept

◆ **Review the "actuals" of your week** and chart it out, dividing it the same as you did in your priorities chart in Step 2.

◆ **Then compare the new priorities chart against your "actuals" chart.** Identify the areas that conflict with what your heart craves right now.

◆ **Finally, take action.** Check below for some tips on how to go about doing it.

Hip Tip   *For a more detailed book that will help you chart your life, check out* LIFE STRATEGIES: DOING WHAT WORKS, DOING WHAT MATTERS *by Phillip C. McGraw.*

Take Your Life Back

◆ **Identify the risks** you'll have to take to achieve your new priorities. Write them down. Change and ambiguity are often scary. It means not being in full control of the outcome. It can mean losing something in order to gain the greater good. Taking risks could also change your entire lifestyle. You may need to take a step back in pay and responsibility to take a step toward your magazine-writing aspirations.

◆ **Get ready, get set, plan.** While your head might be ready, your heart, finances, or immediate friends or family might need a little more time to prepare. Plan as best as you can before taking large risks. Save up any extra funds for a year, or reach out and begin to build new contacts before leaving your current position.

◆ **Now go! Run, Forrest, Run!** Put the wheels in motion to becoming the person you want to be. Live the life you're dreaming of. Only you can make it happen. And you only get one shot at it.

◆ **Set mini-goals with deadlines.** Let these serve as landmarks for achieving your ultimate, overall goal.

◆ **Reward yourself** for meeting your deadlines and mini-goals. Don't overdo it, of course, as you still have a way to go. But, girl, do indulge in a healthy reward like a manicure or pedicure or a cute little top that will put a smile on your face and inspire you to keep trucking forward.

◆ **Evaluate your status.** Re-strategize or re-prioritize if the situation calls for it.

Hip Tip *Overcome procrastination! Why put off something till tomorrow if you can do it today? Check out the books* THE PROCRASTINATOR'S GUIDE TO SUCCESS *by Lynn Lively or* PROCRASTINATION: WHY YOU DO IT, WHAT TO DO ABOUT IT *by Jane Burka and Lenora Yuen. They're oldie but goodie books on how to step it up when you're not in the mood!*

Tactics for Taking on the World Your Way

◆ **Create more time in your life** toward achieving your new priorities. The amount of time in a day isn't going to change, so it's up to you to rearrange how you spend your 24 hours. For instance, perhaps taking a class in pottery or learning to play tennis is something you're dying to try. Why not swap out your TV time for an hour of prime court fun?

Hip Tip *If you work from home, then dress the part. We're not saying a suit is required, but changing out of your flannel p.j.s might help motivate you to get your work done.*

◆ **Find places to compromise.** Cut your hour lunch back to half an hour so you can use the other half to run your errands. Forgo the fun of mowing a front yard and relocate to a smaller pad closer to your job. This will cut your daily commute from two hours to just one and move you nearer the university. It'll also open up five hours a week to take the MBA classes you want.

Hip Tip *Learn to be flexible and go with the flow. Should your life not go exactly as planned, assert the art of compromise and flexibility to see your priorities through. Facing problems that arise with rigidity or purely accommodating others' wishes will rarely help you achieve your own goal of happiness.*

◆ **Double up on priorities.** Has building and nurturing your friends become more of a priority after focusing on your career and getting ahead for the past five years? Well, since you can't quit your day job to pursue your friendships full time (unless, of course, your name is Paris Hilton and that is your job), maybe you'd better maximize your "free" time by enjoying your lunch with new colleagues, or joining a softball team to get both your exercise priority and social desires fulfilled simultaneously.

Hip Tip *Take advantage of your commute. Get that novel you've been meaning to read on CD and listen to it while you're on the road, or play catch-up with the girls. The cell phone companies offer great deals for free minutes during certain hours. If it's during a time you can work it into your schedule, why not talk for free and when it's convenient for you?*

◆ **Delegate responsibilities.** Don't spread yourself so thin, particularly on tasks not important to your happiness. Hire a cleaning lady, an assistant or an intern. Teach your kids responsibility by enlisting them in household chores and cut your vacuuming and dishwashing duties in half. Why feel guilty? Please, girl! Life is short. We need to focus on the things that make us happiest. Sure, teaching your help how to execute the task at hand might be more time-consuming in the beginning, but after a few short trials, it should all run hunky dory. And remember, if your help chooses to wash the dirty laundry before waxing the kitchen floor even though that's not the order you do it in, what's the big deal? As long as the result is to your satisfaction, who cares how she executes it? Don't be a micro-manager. Otherwise you might as well have not bothered delegating in the first place.

Hip Tip *Nobody's perfect so don't think your work always has to be, either. Take stock. How important is it really that your jeans be ironed for your little boy's football game? Don't waste time obsessively perfecting a task when you could be spending the time doing something else. At work, consider having someone else look over your work for you — like a co-worker, friend or sweetie, to help you edit your project before you turn it in. Two eyes are better than one!*

◆ **Learn to measure.** Of course we don't mean for you to run off and enroll in culinary school. But learning to measure exactly what results your boss or client anticipates from your efforts will help you strategize how much effort to put into each paper, meeting and project in order to satisfy their expectations. Sometimes you'll want to raise the bar to impress your clients with something more. But on projects that aren't as important to the company, passenger, client, patient or student, why not simply meet their expectations? Use the extra time you would have spent going above and beyond to join friends for a drink, or make plans with the cutie pie next door to hit the golf course for a few lessons?

◆ **Set boundaries and precedents.** This will manage the expectations of your colleagues, friends and boss who have become accustomed to your work style and standards, and who plan their needs from you around what they know and trust about your behavior. (Of course there will be quarters, seasons, projects and situations that will require you to give more time and effort than normal — from filling in for a waitress who failed to show up, to preparing a solid defense for a really challenging lawsuit. But anticipating the beginning and end to those periods will help you barrel through them. Sucking it up with a positive attitude will show you're loyal to your company.) Below are some areas for you to consider in setting precedents or re-establishing your boundaries at work:

- ☐ Arrival and departure time
- ☐ Working weekends
- ☐ Travel
- ☐ Lunch breaks
- ☐ Vacation time
- ☐ Sick days
- ☐ Work conditions (i.e., office vs. cubicle, available resources, etc.)

Hip Tip *Just pass on the nonessentials! Don't join any committees you aren't truly invested in, unless your boss made it clear (even though she may position it as voluntary) that she'd like for you to consider joining the diversity team. Even then, be a participant, not a leader. Leading a group or sitting on the board involves more time and effort. Also, graciously decline invitations to events that are not a must.*

◆ **Ask for what you want** and say no to what you don't. Be clear. Think about it like this: Your boyfriend won't know that you want that

Banana Republic dress or pair of Seven jeans for your birthday if you don't tell him. Likewise, if your boss is used to your taking on extra work, she won't know that you can't pick up extra shifts this month because you've got a final scheduled.

◆ **Be proactive, not reactive,** with your requests. If you see that you need to end your internship a couple of weeks early, notify your boss immediately. This heads up will give her enough time to readjust her needs accordingly. Or if you want to take a vacation, request it in writing a month in advance if possible. The further in advance you can make it, the fewer hassles you'll encounter — including vacation request overlap with colleagues and last-minute workload responsibilities.

◆ **Whenever possible, show consideration to the company's needs** when making arrangements for your personal needs. Hopefully, this will reinforce your loyalty while still asserting your health as your priority. If you've decided to have that elective knee surgery that will require you to take a month off on short-term disability and your doctor says it's not urgent, talk with your boss about which month would work best in accordance with the company's seasonal workload.

—◄◖◗►—

Indulging in those irresistible mint Girl Scout cookies is heavenly until too much of a good thing has you purging. The same is true in life. Solely focusing on your career doesn't make for a healthy you. Strive to strike a balance in your life. Simultaneously nurture your personal happiness as you focus on your next career move.

Resigning:
Off to Greener Pastures

"My husband was promoted with his job but it required him to relocate to Washington D.C., a move that would take us half-way across the country. I was excited for my husband, but disappointed because my boss and I had really clicked and I really liked where I worked. So when I went in to resign, I was pleasantly surprised that my boss was very supportive and asked me to keep him informed about my job hunt. I still hadn't found anything full-time a few weeks before my husband and I were to leave when one day my supervisor surprised me with great news: My company had created a new position for me in the D.C. office. My new job was a total promotion for me, with an increase in pay and a better title! And now I chuckle at how much anxiety I felt about resigning."

— Alysia, 30, Television News Producer

You've read the "The Big O" chapter of this book, and after much consideration of how it will affect your and your loved ones' futures, you've decided to resign from your position. Depending on your situation, this may be one of the most exciting or frightening opportunities, or both, that you've ever encountered in your life. So here are some tips on how to get through it with confidence and pride.

The "Oral Exam": Resigning In-Person

If you don't have a contract with your employer that says you've got a legal obligation to stay, quitting may be as simple as going in and meeting with your boss. Yeah, we know, we make it sound much easier than it feels. Getting your "oral examination" in a dentist's chair may seem even more appealing than resigning face to face with your boss! So whether you can't wait to "tell her off" or you're petrified of her response, we urge you to read below for making your resignation meeting a peaceful one.

Hip Tip *Keep your lips sealed about your resignation. Don't even tell your most trusted co-workers about your plans to leave the company until you've informed your manager. You never know who might be jockeying for your position before you even resign.*

◆ **Make flashcards or bullet points** of what you're going to say. Practice it, making sure to stick to the topics on your mind. Remember that even if she's the reason you're fleeing, you never want to burn a bridge. You may need her for a reference, or she may run in the same circle as your next supervisor.

Hip Tip *There's a time and place for everything, including resigning. Try to schedule your resignation for late afternoon on a Monday or*

Tuesday, about an hour or two before quitting time. This gives you enough time (but not too much) to talk to your boss and co-workers before the day is done. That way if there is any awkwardness, you both have an entire evening to chill out. Also by notifying your supervisor early in the week, you give her more time to work up a counter-offer with the HR team, if she's so inclined.

◆ **Drop the news gracefully,** sticking to the delivery you practiced at home. Emphasize the positives both about your experience at the firm (no matter if you'd like to tell her where to shove it!), and that this is the best decision for your future. Be prepared for the possibility that your boss may try and probe you for more information, like more specific reasons why you're leaving, where you're going, if you're taking your assistant and so on. Don't be obstructive but simply make it clear that you are submitting an oral resignation, and give a specific date for your last day of employment.

Hip Tip   *The standard resignation calls for two weeks' notice. If you're giving less than that due to other obligations, offer to stay late or work through lunches to help make up for the short notice. If you can, offer more time for your boss to get situated for your departure. Three weeks or a month often makes the transition smoother and leaves your boss with a good impression of you and your work ethic. It's also important to note that some supervisors may take your resignation personally, feel your leaving is disloyal, or fear that you'll take precious client business with you. If that's the case, they will probably ask you to leave immediately or simply leave you out of the loop on further confidential business matters. Therefore, plan as if this may happen and have your ducks in a row for a quick departure before resigning.*

◆ **Expect and prepare for a reaction.** Unless your boss is expecting you to resign or has been practically pushing for it, your decision may come as a surprise to her. She'll likely find the news unsettling. She may get emotional or even confrontational. Remain calm and confident. Stick to your prepared comments. Watch your tone, and don't let it fluctuate even if she becomes hostile or attacking. And most important, stick to your pre-prepared comments. It'll keep you from straying into dangerous, more heated territory.

Hip Tip *Although you've given your company two weeks' notice, it's best to try to continue a strong work ethic and not slack off. Continue to arrive on time or early, and put in a full day's work.*

◆ **First impressions aren't everything.** Last impressions can be equally important. So leave your meeting on a good note and be as cooperative as possible. Thank her for the opportunity to have worked with her and the company; tell her that you learned a great deal (even if all you learned was what qualities you *don't* want in your next supervisor). Also, reinforce that you'll do your best to undertake the handover of any uncompleted work before your departure.

◆ **Discuss and nail down a date** that you can expect to receive any money owed to you, like earned commission or travel and expense reimbursement. If you have accrued vacation, for example you work one year and get two weeks in the second year, you're legally entitled to your accrued vacation time unless you failed to meet a prespecified policy (like you lose your accrued vacation if you fail to give a two-week notice). Also some states have laws that require companies to pay commissions earned before their term date. If there is no such law protecting commissions in your state, then you should definitely request it in your resignation. Know, however, it is within their rights to refuse your request. If you have a contract with the company and want to resign, consult an attorney to see what loopholes exist.

Hip Tip *Some companies or organizations will request that you sign an exit interview form for two purposes: valuable feedback on the company itself and in the event an employee files for unemployment pay. You do not have to sign anything! We recommend that you request to take the form home to review before signing it, where you can give honest responses with a clear mind. You can also decide if you want to have a labor attorney review it before signing, depending on any extenuating circumstances you've encountered. Also, you can complete as much or as little of the form as you choose. You don't work for them anymore and don't have to follow their rules.*

Put it in Writing: Written Resignations

A written letter of resignation can be less stressful in that it gives you greater control of your message and delivery. It also provides clear documentation of your intentions, so that there can be no claim of miscommunication later on.

◆ **A resignation letter should include** your name, date and the name of the person you're addressing, then an opening that offers your notice of termination and when, exactly, you'll be leaving. End with a closing like "Sincerely" or "Yours truly" and your signature.

◆ **If you're leaving under good circumstances** and feel that you want to say a little bit more, again, emphasize the positive — perhaps thank the boss for the opportunities she gave you and the work-related lessons you learned from her. (Now, wouldn't it be nice if all our break-ups could end this peacefully?)

◆ **If you're leaving under tumultuous circumstances,** resist the temptation to accuse, verbally attack or condescend to the boss, both in your letter of resignation and in your follow-up meeting. In particular, never put potentially inflammatory and volatile thoughts and opinions in your resignation letter. Your comments will remain in your personnel file and may come back to haunt you. It also can make getting any money owed to you, like unpaid commissions or travel and expense reimbursements, harder to collect.

◆ **Particularly in cases where you're not leaving in the most ideal of circumstances** — for whatever personal or professional reasons there may be — agree with your boss to the "official" lingo for leaving the company. If you can't agree, involve your HR team. At the same time, agree how and when you should notify co-workers, clients and vendors about your quitting.

HipTip *When speaking to (or emailing) all of your colleagues and associates about your resignation, keep your remarks positive and consistent. Getting loose-lipped (and roaringly ripped) at your going away party is no way to end your good track record at the company. Trust us, even the worst of enemies in a workplace will bond over humiliating stories. Thank them for their contribution to your time at the firm. Try to remain in touch because you never know when they'll be useful to your personal and career development in the future. And most important, don't take it too personally if work acquaintances don't eagerly contact you right after you leave. Times like these are awkward for everyone. They may need your reassurance — like making the first phone call after your departure — that you're interested in maintaining a relationship with them.*

◆ **Request an exit interview with your HR team.** An exit interview process assists the human resources team in determining patterns or trends within a company or department or with a particular supervisor. It also allows for a former employee to communicate problems with supervision, work rules or conditions, and wages discreetly and with someone who has the power to evoke change. Again, you should not entirely let loose with your feelings. Offer specific examples instead. What you say will be forever cemented in writing. Look on this as an opportunity to diplomatically suggest and inspire certain changes for the people who remain. Save your total bad-mouthing for your non-work friends and mates who can agonize with you about the guy in the cubicle beside you who always reeked of unbearable body odor.

Hip Tip *If you're leaving because of illegal activities, such as sexual harassment or discrimination of any kind, an exit interview can serve as documentation of your claims and act as your evidence in case of a pending lawsuit. Request a copy of the exit form for your files before leaving the company, otherwise there is no documentation that the notification took place. You are also entitled to obtain a copy of your personnel files, both while you work for the company and at the time of resignation, and it's best to request it in writing. You may be charged nominal copy fees. Also, know that your personnel file is a legal document that an attorney representing you, the ex-employee, can subpoena on your behalf.*

When You're Oh-So-Good: The Counter-Offer

Girl, you know you're da' bomb, and doesn't it feel oh so good when your boss knows it too? Here's what to do when you quit, but your boss makes a counter-offer:

◆ **Examine the details of what the counter-offer includes:** A higher salary, promotion, relocation, new and more credible accounts, more flex time or a better work schedule, or combination of several of the above? If they're willing to work with you, why not consider staying with them?

◆ **Weigh the pros and cons.** Will what the company is offering you in exchange for your willingness to stay change your reasons for resigning in the first place? More money won't likely replace the respect, value and credit you've been missing for long.

◆ **How does your resignation affect your and your boss's relationship** and morale within the company? If you can't honestly say your commitment will be 100 percent to make the new deal work, don't take it. But if you feel certain about the changes they've offered, then you'll need to respond to their belief in you and reaffirm that you really want to be there.

Hip Tip *Do not cry wolf by resigning in hopes that your company will counter offer. When you decide to resign, expect and prepare for it to be for keeps. Of course we all want to feel loved and valued and therefore would be flattered by any attempt to keep us. But no matter how worthy you are of a counter offer, not everyone is willing to go the extra mile for talent. If that's the case, take pride in knowing you're making the right decision and that you'd never have been happy because they'd never have fully appreciated your talents.*

◆ **If you choose to accept the counter-offer,** ask yourself, how might it affect your integrity with your would-be-employer? Make sure to call the person who offered you the job first. You don't want him to hear the "bad news" through someone other than you. Be delicate, reassuring him that your intentions were pure. Start by thanking him for the opportunity, then emphasize that you were really excited to work with him and for the company but that your current employer countered with an incredible package that you couldn't turn down. Listen to his response. He may be inclined to up the ante with a counter-offer of his own. Girl, if that's the case, seriously consider the offer before giving him an answer. Good for you! You've got yourself an official bidding war. Tell them, "May I have 24 hours to consider your generous offer and let you know by XX time tomorrow?" Immediately notify your current employer of your situation. Then be professional and timely with letting both employers know your final decision as soon as you've decided.

Hip Tip Get any final counter offers in writing, even if it's just in an email. You'd hate to agree to certain perks and then be told later that they were never part of the deal or came with clauses. You can initiate a written offer casually by drafting an email that reads: "Susan, just to clarify what you're offering, I get an additional five paid vacation days (totaling 25 paid vacation days per year) and a $10,000 raise. Is that correct?" Also, depending on your level in the department, consider getting an attorney or agent to negotiate your counter offers for you. See the "Nailing the Negotiations" chapter for more on that.

Resignation Examples

Following are several sample written letters of resignation which we pulled from www.i-resign.com. The letters we extracted offer several reasons for quitting. For more personalized formats to consider when turning in your letter of resignation, check out their Website.

LETTER 1:

Dear *<the recipient's name goes here>*:

I write to confirm that I am resigning from my position as *<your job title goes here>*.

Although there is no written contract of employment between us, I accept that we have a verbal agreement and that my notice period stands at *<your notice period goes here>* weeks. Please be assured that I will do all I can to assist in the smooth transfer of my responsibilities before leaving.

I wish both you and *<the name of your current employer goes here>* every good fortune and I would like to thank you for having me as part of your team.

Yours sincerely,
<your signature>

LETTER 2:

Dear *<the recipient's name goes here>*:

As required by my contract of employment, I hereby give you *<your notice period goes here>* weeks' notice of my intention to leave my position as *<your job title goes here>*.

I wish both you and *<the name of your current employer goes here>* every good fortune and I would like to thank you for having me as part of your team.

Yours sincerely,
<your signature>

L<small>ETTER</small> 3:

Dear *<the recipient's name goes here>*:

As required by my contract of employment, I hereby give you *<your notice period goes here>* weeks' notice of my intention to leave my position as *<your job title goes here>*.

I have decided that it is time to move on and I have accepted a position elsewhere. This was not an easy decision and took a lot of consideration. However, I am confident that my new role will help me to move toward some of the goals I have for my career.

Please be assured that I will do all I can to assist in the smooth transfer of my responsibilities before leaving.

I wish both you and *<the name of your current employer goes here>* every good fortune and I would like to thank you for having me as part of your team.

Yours sincerely,
<your signature>

Whether in love or in work, leaving is never easy. But it's a lot more empowering to reject than to be rejected. So be sensitive to the other person's feelings while satisfying your needs.

The Pink Slip:
Victoria's Ugly Secret

———————

"I learned that my school district was having 'budgetary problems.' I didn't think I had anything to worry about since I had seniority over so many others. Boy was I wrong! Four hundred and twenty pink slips later, yours truly was jobless come next semester. Devastated and depressed, I went home and isolated myself in my dark room for days, even calling in sick to work. Thank heaven for my roommate, who finally barged in and barred me from playing one more sappy "Journey" love song. She set me straight, "Get a hold of yourself! You lost your job, not your boyfriend." She was right. My heart wasn't broken, just my luck. And just as I was getting back on my feet, turns out the school ended up needing me to stay after all."

— Joy, 28, 1st grade teacher

Perhaps you could see doomsday coming, or maybe it feels like you've just been struck by lightning. Either way, being laid off or fired from your job can feel humiliating and frightening. But since a

Hip Girl knows that her job doesn't constitute her worth, hold your head up high and chalk this one up to a learning experience. With time and persistence, you might even find that being let go was a blessing in disguise. Read below for more on how to carry off your pink-slip saga with success.

Forecasting a Lay-off

Okay, if you're one of the lucky ones, you'll see the storm coming. Do what any Hip Girl would do to weather a storm — prepare for torrential showers. Here are some tips that might help you spot a potential lay-off or firing:

◆ **You've been warned at least once verbally** and in writing about your job performance or placed on probation. This could be due to anything from consistently low sales, repeated tardiness, poor management skills (like screaming and hollering at your subordinates), improper office behavior or practices, and so on. It's up to your employer to determine what behavior is appropriate for your office (unless, of course, it's an illegal reason you've been fired like race, sex, religion, gender, age, pregnancy, etc. Check out the "Foreplay for Fairplay" chapter for more details on this).

◆ **You read in the newspaper or industry trade magazine** that statewide government cutbacks are imminent or your industry is rapidly declining, like when the dot-com boom crashed.

◆ **Your company is consistently dropping massive points** in the stock market over a long period of time.

◆ **Your boss's boss starts shooting off memos regularly** about the company's "new direction" or "mission."

◆ **You're about to be acquired by another, larger organization.**

◆ **Various branches or stores across the country are quickly closing.**

◆ **You have all new management** or a new supervisor who's clearly trying to make your day-to-day job a living hell so that you'll quit.

◆ **New technology is reducing the number of live people** it requires to run the equipment.

◆ **Your workload is cut in half** or your responsibilities shift from top-level priorities to lower-rung activities.

◆ **Your boss asks you to consider a pay decrease or demotion.**

◆ **Your temporary replacement or substitute has been asked to stay indefinitely** even though you've returned to your job full-time and you can't see where more work has been added to require a whole new position.

◆ **The overall country's economic climate is falling drastically.**

◆ **A traumatic or disastrous event** becomes the impetus for a trickle-down cause-and-effect firing.

◆ **The good ol' gossip mill keeps coming back with the same rumor.** Don't let it haunt you. Instead, get in front of the rumor.

Protection: It's Your Number One Safety Mechanism for Landing on Your Feet

Just like it's important to arm yourself with know-how against unforeseen trouble on a road trip to Palm Springs with the girls, it's equally important to protect your future by preparing for an unexpected layoff or firing. Here are some suggestions of what to do before you get the ax:

◆ **Build a nest egg of liquid funds.** Maybe you're living paycheck to paycheck, or as your paycheck grew, so did your spending. Either way, socking a portion of each paycheck into a savings account or mutual fund is important to safeguard yourself (and your lifestyle) from a potential loss of income. Check out the "Show Me the Money" chapter of *The Hip Girl's Handbook for Home, Car & Money Stuff* to help you budget what you make so that you can save enough for the "rainy day."

◆ **Rearrange your future savings priorities.** Don't give into temptation to take your money out of your 401(k). You'll suffer huge tax penalties for doing that, which aren't worth the headache. Instead, look into setting up a personal IRA that you can roll your money into, or leave your money in there until you get another job. That way you can simply roll it over into your new company's 401(k) plan. For more information on 401(k) and retirement plans, check out www.irs.gov, or consult a certified financial advisor.

Hip Tip *If you're laid off, fired or you resign, whatever portion of your corporate stock is vested is legally yours and in no way can be garnished upon your departure. The federal law that enforces this policy is the Employee Retirement Income Security Act (ERISA). Check out the HR section of this book for more information on pension plans.*

◆ **Update your résumé, quick.** Then start putting it out there for the world to see. (Check out "The Basics," "What Now?" and "Big 'O'" chapters for more on re-entering the world of looking for a job.)

Hip Tip *You should always keep your résumé updated with your most recent job experience, responsibilities and contact information. If your title or responsibilities change, make it a point to change the information on your résumé the same day. Otherwise, you're likely to put it off to another day, which may come too late.*

◆ **Reacquaint yourself with everyone** and anyone you've dealt with in your career who could potentially help you find a new job. And if you can write the lunch or drinks off to your current employer because they're in some way connected to your current position (like as a potential client or vendor), then all the more power to you, girl! That-a-way to ethically "stretch" the company dollar to your benefit!

◆ **Utilize the freebies your company offers** to help you manage your unemployment future. Does your company have a life-career counselor on staff to help you determine your career direction before you're let go? Save money: Eat the company's catered lunches, drink their coffee (instead of getting your fancy latte from your favorite coffee spot) or cancel your gym membership and use the one provided by the company. You get the drift.

◆ **Take care of health procedures and dental check-ups.** You might as well get your operation and rehabilitation paid for. Put those benefits to work for you . . . while you can still get a good portion of them paid for you. (For more specifics on your work employment benefits, see the "Human Resources Breakdown" chapter.)

◆ **Take unused paid vacation or personal time** if you won't be paid for it when you're laid off. Also, we know you're a conscientious employee who rarely takes off work even when you're on your death bed, but why not consider taking some of that unused paid sick leave to interview for your next gig?

◆ **Update your portfolio** with proof of your most stellar performances (like your brilliant advertisement layout, press release or science plan) and make sure your Palm Pilot contains current contact information. Don't take any information, documents or property that might be considered confidential or potentially illegal for you to take. Maintaining your ethical behavior in the workplace is never more important than when you're exiting the company.

◆ **Discreetly and intermittently remove personal things from your office.** If you've got a big poster-size portrait of your family hanging in your cubicle or office, don't remove it; that makes it painfully obvious you're "checking out" mentally before your company forces you out. However, if you've stored some personal things on your company's computer or Palm Pilot (which, let us reinforce again, is a bad idea), or you've got your personal finance documents stashed in your filing cabinet (again, not a good place for these), get 'em out *fast!* Stay late or take your lunch hour to transfer that stuff to a disc. Once companies decide your tenure is over and done with, they take no time getting you outta' there. There isn't usually an opportunity to go back and get your belongings. Just remember, make your transfer as unobvious as possible so as not to tip them off to the fact that you're already two steps ahead of them.

◆ **Keep a positive and professional demeanor** whenever dealing with anyone related to your career, including vendors, clients, supervisors and colleagues. Exiting with grace and dignity should be your mantra. Don't storm out throwing a temper tantrum. You'll want to keep them for referrals in the future.

Tick Tock, Your Time is Up

If you've been fired or laid off, how do you handle it and what do you do now?

◆ **Maintain your professional behavior.** Once again, you'll want to leave with dignity. This could allow you to use your boss or HR representative for a referral for future employment opportunities.

Hip Tip *Don't fret if your employer monitors your departure. As odd as it may sound, it's actually a common practice for companies to have a human resources or security staff member accompany laid-off workers to their desks. Your "escort" should wait while you pack up your belongings, then assist you out of the office. Don't take the notion of an escort personally. It doesn't mean they think you're a criminal. Large companies just follow these operating procedures for their own protection from possible lawsuits. Smaller companies tend to not be quite as procedural with their dismissals. Make sure you maintain your professional demeanor at all times, even if your boss isn't necessarily doing the same.*

◆ **Request specific feedback.** Under different circumstances, is there a possibility for re-employment? Inquire what areas you can improve upon in your new job. What exactly will your severance package consist of?

Hip Tip *Do not beg for your job back! If your employer is clearly saying you're fired or laid off, hold your head high and take it like a lady. Hip Girls don't beg for anything! The word "desperate" isn't even in our vocabulary.*

◆ **Request and agree to a story** that you can offer your colleagues, clients and future employer about your untimely departure. In the event of a lay-off, the best way to broach the subject with a potential new employer is to attribute your lay-off to a corporate downsizing, elimination of your position or change in your industry's economic climate. Conversely, if you've been fired specifically because of a work performance issue, see if your former employer will back you up on one of the following stories: "I needed a new challenge," or "There was little room for growth" or "I've always been passionate about cooking or (fill in the blank) and I finally decided it was time to pursue it full-time." If not, offer a broad-based truth in the most positive light. Spin it in a way that may make someone more compassionate toward your situation, then clearly state how you've overcome the plight. For instance, if you repeatedly missed work, were late and rarely prepared to tackle the day owing to marital problems, instead of being specific about your downfall, simply say, "I was going through a difficult divorce and work wasn't my priority." Reassure them it's no longer an issue and that you're anxious for a fresh start.

◆ **Agree how you'll let your colleagues, clients and vendors know** about your leaving the company. Should you send a mass email, tell a few people on your way out or just leave quietly.

Hip Tip *Be brief, polite and sincere if you decide mass email is your best bet for notifying people of your departure. Just give your new contact information (if you wish), thank them for the opportunity to have worked together, and wish them well in their own endeavors.*

◆ **Discreetly and quickly grab your belongings.** Even if you're given the opportunity to take your time — from an afternoon to a couple of weeks — to collect your things, consider the awkwardness for both you and others if you hang out at the office knowing you're really not wanted anymore. Do you ride out the humility in exchange for utilizing the company's resources for finding your next potential employer? Can your ego take it and all the behind-your-back stares and snickering about what really happened?

Storming the Aftermath — What to Do Right After You've Faced the Firing Range

◆ **Keep your chin up.** Believe in yourself and that this is truly a good test to learn just how much of a survivor you really are.

Hip Tip *Ever consider teaching? Across the country, large cities scramble to hire professionals to teach in city schools. Contact Teach For America at www.teachforamerica.org or your local public school system. If you're not ready to take on that much of a commitment, look into becoming a substitute teacher. It may just be the perfect way for you to earn some extra money while still looking for a job. Who knows? You just might find an all-new passion.*

◆ **Review your employee benefits packet.** Empower yourself by asserting your rights. Know what your company's responsibility is to you during this time. If you're fully vested, do they have to cash you out of your stock options? If you've got leftover sick leave or paid vacation time, do they owe you for it? Do you have a contract that says despite a force-out, they have to buy you out of the duration of your contract? Consult an attorney if you meet resistance from the HR representative or supervisor who's denying you your rights.

Hip Tip *The Website www.legal-database.com helps explain different employment law issues for a clearer understanding of what your legal rights* might be. You may seriously want to consider getting an attorney if you feel you've been illegally let go. Just make sure to look for an attorney in your area that specializes in employment, workplace or labor law issues. The yellow pages of your local telephone book will probably be your best resource. Look under "law" or "attorney." If their ad doesn't say what the firm specializes in, call and inquire. Sometimes the best way to find an attorney is to get references from your family and friends.

◆ **Rearrange your budget** to accommodate a three-to-six month "low cash flow" period. Check out the "Show Me the Money" chapter in *"The Hip Girl's Handbook for Home, Car & Money Stuff"* to help you come up with a budget that fits your new Lucky Charms cereal meals lifestyle. Some strategies to consider are saving up your job-search receipts for a tax write-off come April 12, or lowering your auto insurance rates to a no-work mileage grace period.

◆ **Check into your health and dental insurance coverage options** during your unemployment. At age 20, you may not think having health insurance is all that much of a priority. Yeah, well, these Hip Girls can't even begin to tell you how many times we now realized that we (and our friends) were lucky gals. For instance, during a drunken state, one of our dearest friends fell off a moving trolley we'd rented for our Fourth of July celebration. Fortunately, she just suffered bumps and scrapes. But it just goes to show that health-related incidents can pop up at any age.

Hip Tip   The Consolidated Omnibus Budget Reconciliation Act (COBRA) is a federal law that allows you to continue your health care coverage after you leave your job. Your company's responsibility to cover your COBRA benefits normally runs out 60 days after you leave a job. Out-of-pocket COBRA costs tend to be quite expensive. Amounts vary depending upon the type of coverage you want and length of time you want it. Log on to www.cobrainsurance.com to find out more information about COBRA.

◆ **Build a support system.** Getting laid-off or fired from our jobs often makes us feel incredibly vulnerable. Turn to your friends, family, spouse or a therapist for an ear to listen and take your mind off your problems. Sometimes, ain't nothin' going to cure your blues better than just getting all dolled up and going out and dancing your bootie off.

◆ **Check into your unemployment check options.** Do you file for unemployment? That's up to you. We say you pay for them regardless, so why not reap the benefits when you need them? In our opinion, it's only when you take advantage of the system (like to finance your trip to Spain during your unemployment) that it raises a concern about your priorities. On the other hand, we respect that some gals have great difficulty filing for unemployment. We say do what is right for you.

Hip Tip *For more information on unemployment eligibility and how to file it in your state, log onto www.dol.gov and search by topic under "unemployment insurance," call 1-866-4-USA-DOL (1-866-487-2365), or go to your local employment office. Also note that in case you suffer from prolonged unemployment, you do have the option to file an extension. Check the Website above for additional information on extensions.*

◆ **Re-evaluate your career aspirations.** Don't just leap into your next job out of fear and desperation. Take time to consider if your current career path makes you happy. Do you want to go back to graduate school? How about changing fields? Check out the "What Now?" and "Off to Greener Pastures" chapters for more guidance. Also, perhaps now is a great time to consult a career counselor if you're grappling with mapping out your professional future. If push comes to shove and you absolutely need money, you can take a low-responsibility, part-time position (like as a barista, bartender, phone or sales clerk) to just get you by while you look for the job that will get you one step closer to your dream position.

Hip Tip *Get physical. Now is the perfect time to hit the gym (if you can still afford the membership) or learn the cardio workout courtesy of the good ol' outdoors. Not only will it help you get rid of some of your work-induced weight, it's a great way to fight depression, which can only drag you down while you're trying to pump yourself up to deal with future employers.*

◆ **Finally, devise a day-by-day plan** that gets you up and going in search of your new and exciting job. Check out "The Basics" chapter for step-by-step instructions for launching your efforts methodically. Strategize and organize your efforts to get you where you're going (and to remember where you've been) and what your follow-up steps will require to snag the career you've always dreamed of.

———※———

In today's high-stakes, high-turnover world, getting the boot from your employer is practically a rite of passage for climbing the career ladder. Girl, now that you've earned your unemployment stripes, get out there and show 'em you're a survivor!

Hip Girls Walk the Walk

As you begin to outline your plan of attack for launching, navigating or transitioning your career, remember that no career decision is wrong so long as you've learned from the experience.

The only bad choice is feeling stuck in a position that consistently leaves you unfulfilled and dependent on someone else for your happiness. Happiness can only come from within. You can't rely solely on your husband, material things, career or kids to bring you everlasting, inner peace. Please! That's like suggesting one pair of shoes could meet your needs for every outfit. So just as it takes numerous pairs of shoes to fit our ever-changing fashion moods, so too does it take fully developing, nurturing and balancing the various parts of you as an individual, wife, mother, career woman, sister, aunt and daughter.

That's not to suggest that these exterior elements can't bring you years of joy. But they can't fill a void rooted deep inside you. You must first be happy with yourself and pleased with where you're headed. Then, and only then, should you look for people and things that add to your happiness!

Now buckle up those stilettos, ladies, and continue to walk the walk of your professional journey. If your heel breaks along the way, let your spirit catch you. Then just kick both heels off and run barefoot toward the goal that drives you, letting the pain from the blisters and bruises motivate you. Once you get where you're going — even if you land in a destination other than you'd planned — remember to relish your path because no one else could have done it quite the way you did!

Resources

Books and Articles

Arbetter, Lisa. *Secrets of Style: InStyle's Complete Guide to Dressing Your Very Best Every Day.* New York, NY: Time, 2003.

Berg, Rona. *Beauty, The New Basic.* New York, NY: Workman Publishing, 2001.

Bolles, Richard Nelson. *What Color Is Your Parachute? A Practical Manual for Job-Hunters and Career-Changers.* Berkeley, CA: Ten Speed Press, 2003.

Diresta, Diane. *Knockout Presentations: How to Deliver Your Message with Power, Punch, and Pizzazz.* Worcester, MA: Chandler House Press, 1998.

Dorio, Marc. *The Complete Idiot's Guide to The Perfect Interview, Second Edition.* Indianapolis, IN: Alpha Books, 2000.

Etiquette girls. *Things You Need to be Told.* New York, NY: Berkley Books, 2001.

Falcone, Paul. *The Hiring and Firing Question and Answer Book.* New York, NY: American Management Association, 2001.

Farr, Kendall. *The Pocket Stylist: Behind the Scenes Expertise from a Fashion Pro on Creating Your Own Unique Look.* New York, NY: Gotham, 2004.

Fifield, Kathleen. "Works for Me." *InStyle.* October, 2003.

Fox, Jeffrey J. *Don't Send a Résumé: And Other Contrarian Rules to Help Land a Great Job.* New York, NY: Hyperion, 2001.

France, Kim and Andrea Linett. *The Lucky Shopping Manual: Building and Improving Your Wardrobe Piece by Piece.* New York, NY: Gotham, 2003.

Frankel, Lois P. *Nice Girls Don't Get the Corner Office: 101 Unconscious Mistakes Women Make to Sabotage their Careers.* New York, NY: Warner Books, 2004.

Friedman, Caitlin and Kimberly Yorio. *The Girl's Guide to Starting Your Own Business: Candid Advice, Frank Talk, and True Stories for the Successful Entrepreneur.* New York, NY: Harper Resource, 2003.

Johnson, Tony, Robyn Freedman Spizman, Lindsey Pollak. *Women For Hire: The Ultimate Guide to Getting a Job.* New York, NY: Perigee Books, 2002.

Lively, Lynn. *Procrastinator's Guide to Success.* New York, NY: McGraw-Hill, 1999.

Macko, Lia and Kerry Rubin. *Midlife Crisis at 30: How the Stakes have Changed for a New Generation — and What to Do About It.* New York, NY: Rodale Publishing, 2004.

McGraw, Phillip C. *Life Strategies: Doing What Works, Doing What Matters.* New York, NY: Hyperion, 2000.

McKinney, Anne. *Real-Résumés for Sale.* Fayetteville, NC: Prep Publishing, 2000.

Messmer, Max. *Job Hunting for Dummies.* New York, NY: Hungry Minds, 1999.

Moses, Barbara, Ph. D. *What Next? The Complete Guide to Taking Control of Your Working Life.* New York, NY: DK Publishing Inc, 2003.

Musselman, Jennifer and Patty DeGregori. *The Hip Girl's Handbook for Home, Car and Money Stuff.* Tulsa, OK: Wildcat Canyon Press, 2001.

Nadler, Burton Jay. *The Everything Resume Book: Great Resumes for Every Situation 2nd Edition.* Avon, MA: Adams Media Corporation, 2003.

O'Connell, Brian. *The Career Survival Guide: Making Your Next Career Move.* New York, NY: McGraw-Hill, 2003.

Renckly, Richard G. *Human Resources.* Hauppauge, NY: Barron's, 2004.

Skinner, Anna. *How to Pee Standing Up: Tips for Hip Chicks.* New York, NY: Downtown Press, 2003.

Solovic, Susan Wilson. *The Girl's Guide to Power and Success.* New York, NY: American Management Association, 2001.

Tracy, Brian. *Get Paid More and Promoted Faster: 21 Great Ways to Get Ahead in Your Career.* San Francisco, CA: Berrett-Koehler Publishers, 2001.

Wellington, Sheila. *Be Your Own Mentor: Strategies from Top Women on the Secrets of Success.* New York, NY: Random House, 2001.

Yuen, Lenora. *Procrastination: Why You Do It, What to Do About It.* New York, NY: Addison Wesley Publishing, 1990.

Websites

Business Women's Network: www.bwni.com

Career Advantage: www.careeradvantage.org

Career Builder: www.careerbuilder.com

Career Fairs: www.careerfairs.com

Center for Businesswoman's Research: www.womensbusinessresearch.org

COBRA Insurance: www.cobrainsurance.com

College Board: www.collegeboard.com

Craig's List: www.craigslist.com

DeGregori, Gormsen & Ringer, LLP: www.dgr-cpas.com

Dress for Success: www.DressforSuccess.org

Equal Employment Opportunity Commission: www.eeoc.gov

Equal Rights Advocates: www.equalrights.org

Employment Development Department: www.edd.ca.gov

Federal Bureau of Investigation: www.fbi.gov

Federal Job Search: www.governmentjobsearch.com

Federal Student Aid (FSA): http://studentaid.ed.gov

FedWorld: www.fedworld.gov

JobStar: www.jobstar.org

InternWeb: www.internweb.com

Internal Revenue Service: www.irs.gov

I-Resign: www.i-resign.com

IVillage: www.ivillage.com

Legal Database: www.legal-database.com

Marshall Field's: www.marshallfields.com

Monster Career Advice: http://content.monster.com

MonsterTrak: www.monstertrak.monster.com

National Association for Female Executives (NAFE): www.NAFE.com

National Career Development Association: www.ncda.org

Nordstroms: www.nordstroms.com

Saks Fifth Avenue: www.saksfifthavenue.com

Showbiz Jobs: www.showbizjobs.com

Student Gov: www.students.gov

Texas A&M University: www.tamu.edu

The Breast Site: www.thebreatsite.com

TRACOM Group: www.tracomcorp.com

Trade Schools Guide: www.trade-schools.net

U.S. Department of Labor : www.dol.gov

Wage Web: www.wageweb.com

WetFeet: www.wetfeet.com

Working Mother: www.workingwoman.com

Yahoo! Hotjobs: http://hotjobs.yahoo.com

Jennifer Musselman *(right)* has climbed — and sometimes tripped — up the corporate ladder at MTV Network's Nickelodeon TV where she is Director of Communications and actively supervises her depart-ment's interns. Prior to joining Nickelodeon, Musselman launched her media career as an unpaid intern at Fox's KTTV Television News before being hired as a field producer and researcher. Before packing up her '93 Dodge Shadow with all her belongings and heading west to pursue her life-long big-business aspirations, she earned her BA in Communications from the University of Northern Iowa.

Patty Fletcher *(left)* is a teacher in Burlingame, California, where she currently resides as a newly married HipGirl. She has a BA degree from Chico State University where she also gained invaluable social and life skills as a sorority sister, waitress and in retail sales. Drawing on her own experiences, she counsels young people on their studies and living issues. Fletcher attended graduate school at California's University of San Diego.